EDINBURGH
EDUCATION AND SOCIETY
SERIES
General Editor: Colin Bell

TO TRISHA, TOM, JACK AND THE LATE LOUISE

Growing up in a Classless Society?

School to work transitions

ANDY FURLONG

EDINBURGH UNIVERSITY PRESS

© Edinburgh University Press, 1992

Edinburgh University Press
22 George Square, Edinburgh

Set in Linotron Palatino
by Koinonia Ltd, Bury, and
printed in Great Britain by
Hartnoll Ltd, Bodmin

A CIP record for this book is
available from the British Library

ISBN 0 7486 0337 9

CONTENTS

FIGURES

TABLES

ACKNOWLEDGEMENTS

I started writing this book while working as a Research Fellow at the Centre for Educational Sociology, University of Edinburgh on the 'Young People's Routes into and within the Labour Market' project. Much of the material included here was first analysed in the context of that project and owes a lot to my colleagues on the project, David Raffe and Peter Ritchie. David Raffe also read the draft manuscript in its entirety and made many invaluable comments and constructive criticisms. I am also indebted to the team at Mackie House who administer the CES surveys, and code and enter the data.

The book also draws on earlier work developed for my Ph.D. at Leicester University which benefited immensely from the guidance and support of Professor David Ashton, Malcolm Maguire and other members of the Centre for Labour Market Studies. Much of the thinking behind this book was inspired by discussions with David Ashton who also read an earlier draft of the manuscript.

The series editor, Professor Colin Bell, also read the manuscript and made helpful comments. I am grateful to my co-authors on a number of papers which have been used here: Rosie Campbell, George Cooney, David Raffe, Ken Roberts and Michael Spearman. Resources for the completion of the book were made available by the Department of Government, University of Strathclyde, and Grace Hunter spent many hours preparing the Tables for the book.

Thanks also to Trisha Furlong for putting up with my evenings in front of the computer screen and to Susan MacIver for finding most of my grammatical errors.

ANDY FURLONG
University of Strathclyde

1

YOUNG PEOPLE AND THE TRANSITION FROM SCHOOL

1.1 Introduction

The generation of young people who left school over the last decade have made their transition to adulthood under the shadow of unemployment and under a political regime which has removed many of the economic safety nets which existed for those growing up in more prosperous periods. Under the threat of withdrawal of benefits, many young people have been forced to contend with various work experience and training schemes set up by the Government, while others have temporarily avoided the turmoil of the declining youth labour market by staying on at school or by entering further education.

As young people become adults they begin to loosen the chains of material dependence which tie them to their families of origin and start to be held responsible for their own material circumstances. The process of becoming an adult is often quite protracted and is not something which happens automatically upon reaching the age of majority. Throughout this century, young people from middle-class families have often been economically dependent on their families until their early twenties, when they finished their university or college courses. On the other hand, many of those from working-class families entered the labour market at the end of compulsory schooling and have been financially independent at a younger age.

This pattern has changed somewhat over the last decade as youth unemployment, training schemes, and increasing levels of participation in post-compulsory education and training have delayed the achievement of economic independence for a whole generation of young people. Roberts (1985) suggests that for those who experience higher education, economic independence has for a long time been the final stage in the transition to adulthood, but that in the 1980s this pattern became a mass phenomenon.

Historically the relationship between age and independence

has tended to reflect economic conditions: indeed, it has been argued that the phase we now call adolescence did not exist in medieval society (Tuchman, 1980), and that 'youth' is socially created and historically variable in the same way as childhood is (Aries, 1962). In medieval society young people were accepted as adults once they reached physical maturity (Tuchman, 1980). In contrast, Springhall has argued that in feudal society young people commonly existed in a dependent state well into their twenties. He suggests that 'an extended period of "youth" was common from the Fifteenth to the Seventeenth Centuries, when some village "boys" in England and France did not marry until their mid-twenties or even later … The young in the early modern period passed through a lengthy period of semi-dependence as servants and apprentices' (Springhall, 1983, p. 21). Youth as a period of semi-dependence preceded industrialisation, and initially the factory system in Britain led to a drastic reduction in the dependent years of youth and the age at which young people married. An important reason for this was that migration to the towns enabled young people to marry at an earlier age because they no longer needed to wait until they inherited property or farming rights (Gillis, 1981).

In the early period of industrialisation (from around the 1780s up until the 1860s), young people's status within the labour market entered a 'golden age'. In the new industries parents were often appendages of their children and were quite frequently dependent upon their offspring's earnings. Musgrove (1964) argued that, in London, girls of fourteen were able to command relatively high earnings ('as much as eight or ten shillings per week'), and 'if they had cause to be dissatisfied with the conduct of their parents, they would leave them' (pp. 67-8). Musgrove suggests that when farm labourers moved to the new towns with their families, this was quite often in pursuit of the potential earnings of their children in the new industrial centres. Indeed, the father was often only able to gain marginal employment. In this period, 'young people, particularly the working class young, were able to approximate to adult status because of their importance to the economy' (Musgrove, 1964, p. 76).

It was during the early period of industrialisation that 'youth' started to be seen as a distinct group of people. The breakdown of the household economy and the increasing importance of wage labour meant that youths began to enjoy some 'freetime' outside of their work and family. (This is likely to have applied less to females who would have been expected to spend much of their 'freetime' on household chores.) With the development of new industries, the concentration of people in the towns also meant that young people became a more conspicuous group (Wallace, 1988). The movement from rural employment and domestic labour into the factories also had important repercussions for young people from upper- and middle-class families. Prior to the 1830s these young people tended to share a similar status to the servants and apprentices in the household. After the 1830s, domestic education declined as the reformed public schools increased in popularity (Musgrove, 1960). In the new public schools, the young enjoyed a status and importance they previously lacked (Musgrove, 1964).

In the latter half of the nineteenth century a new phase of youth dependence came about which led to the emergence of modern youth. According to Biddle (1983), two key movements set the scene for the re-establishment of an extended period of youth dependence. Firstly, increased mechanisation brought about a decline in the need for manual labour. It has been argued that it was only when the need for employing children in industry had elapsed, that laws prohibiting child labour were introduced (Musgrove, 1964). Secondly, there was a move towards compulsory public education which was brought about both by the need for a more highly educated workforce, and through middle-class concerns about morality (Fraser, 1973). Automation and industrial reorganisation plunged youth into a new period of dependence and led to their removal from manufacturing industry and their placement in compulsory education.

Throughout the twentieth century the economic importance of youth declined. By the middle of the century the exclusion of youth from economic activity was more or less complete. By then, Biddle says, 'most Western societies had large groups of post-pubertal citizens, youths, who were separated from adult society in academies, and were denied access to full-time employment and other privileges of adult status' (Biddle, 1983, p. 154). This trend was not as marked in Britain as in the USA. In North America, the institutional provision was such that a much larger percentage of young people remained in education for longer periods than was the case in Britain (Osterman, 1980).

Social scientists have studied 'youth' and the transition to adulthood with varying degrees of intensity since Rousseau in the eighteenth century. The study of youth gained momentum in the early part of the twentieth century after the publication of a number of prominent works by psychologists, and because of middle-class fears about emerging youth cultures (Pearson, 1983). The term 'adolescence' was coined by G. Stanley Hall[1] in the 1880s and it came into common usage after the publication, in 1904, of his mammoth two volume work *Adolescence: Its Psychology and Its Relation to Physiology, Anthropology, Sociology, Sex, Crime, Religion and Education*. Essentially 'adolescence' was a psychological term which was linked to the onset of puberty and development of sexuality. Stanley Hall regarded adolescence as a troubled period in which young people came to terms with physiological changes. Subsequent psychologists have also tended to regard adolescence as a period of 'storm and stress': Erikson (1968), for example, has been influential in portraying adolescence as a period of crisis in which young people develop and confirm their identities. Sociologists and anthropologists have reacted strongly to the view implied by many psychologists that adolescence is a universally stressful period. Perhaps most well known of these critiques is Margaret Mead's (1928) study *Coming of Age in Samoa* in which she argues that adolescent experiences are culturally determined. However, while Mead painted a rosy picture of the life of Samoan adolescents (which has since been criticised by Freeman, (1984)), she contrasted this with the stressful adolescence experienced by young people in America.

The view of adolescence in western society as a difficult period in the lifecycle was common in sociology up until the late 1960s. Millar and Form (1951), for example, regarded the transition from school to work as a stressful period in a young person's life. As young people made the move from school to work, it was argued, they encountered 'considerable frustration' as their previous aspirations were 'beaten down' to fit the realities of the occupational world. During the 1970s, sociologists started to take a broader perspective than had been the case previously and began to study the youth transition as a process central to the reproduction and confirmation of class-based inequalities (for example, Ashton, 1973; Ashton and Field, 1976; Willis, 1977). It is perhaps significant that British sociologists began to regard the transition from school to work as a relatively stress-free period at a time when the economy was buoyant and young people were having little difficulty in finding work after they left school.

Ashton and Field (1976) argued that the the transition from school to work was relatively smooth because of the strength of the process of socialisation. Most young people internalised the normative orientations of their families and these were reinforced by future experiences. Thus young people from working-class families tended to move through the lower streams at school towards less skilled jobs, while those from middle-class families tended to move through the higher streams towards 'career' jobs. As a result of their experiences at home and at school, young people who entered 'middle-class careers' often regarded their work as a central area of achievement and judged their own worth in terms of their career success. In contrast, unskilled workers came to regard work instrumentally as a means of providing resources to enjoy their lives outside the work environment. Ashton and Field recognised that in cases where young people's experiences conflicted with their expectations (as in the case of a boy from middle-class family who attended a grammar school and subsequently worked on the factory floor), then the transition to work may be experienced as a 'traumatic' event.

It may seem somewhat paradoxical that sociologists were starting to regard the transition from school to work as a relatively smooth process for the majority at a time when media attention was fixed on what they regarded as the rebelliousness of contemporary youth. Qualitative sociologists such as Hall and Jefferson (1976) and Willis (1977) were providing illuminating accounts of the significance of youth subcultures and of young people's resistance to 'authority', yet were regarding this resistance as being part of a process which made the transition to work *less* traumatic as young people effectively participated in their own 'self-damnation' and embraced subordinate positions within capitalist society.

For Willis (1977), working-class 'kids' (by which he means males) get working-class jobs because they do not regard manual labour as 'failure'. On the contrary, manual labour is seen as a way in which they can 'prove' their masculinity, and it provides them with an opportunity to oppose the authority and values of the school. On the other hand, 'mental' work tends not to be sought by working class 'kids' because of the perceived need for obedience and conformity: 'working class kids creatively develop, transform and finally reproduce aspects of the larger culture in their own praxis in such a way as to finally direct them to certain kinds of work ... However, this damnation is experienced, paradoxically, as true learning, affirmation, appropriation, and as a form of resistance' (Willis, 1977, pp. 2-3). Willis regards this reaction as a partial 'penetration' of the system of class domination and subordination. In other words, young people gain partial awareness of the nature of class conflict under capitalism in so far as they see the opposition of manual labour and the 'mental' labour which serves the interests of 'authority' (the ruling class) and see themselves as members of the working class.

Hall and Jefferson (1976) take a similar view in so far as youth subcultures reflect class relations. The subculture is 'related to the parent culture of which they are a subset' (p. 13). Again the way in which young people's resistance legitimises the social order is seen as a reflection of the hegemonic nature of class domination within capitalism. This hegemony 'involves the exercise of a special kind of power, the power to win and shape consent, so that the granting of legitimacy appears not only "spontaneous" but natural and normal' (Gramsci, 1971, quoted in Hall and Jefferson, 1976, p. 13).

In sum, sociologists like Ashton and Field, Hall and Jefferson, and Willis regard the transition from school to work as being relatively smooth because by the time young people leave school, they are strongly prepared for the positions they are about to enter in the labour market. Indeed, they regard the entry to these sorts of jobs as completely normal and experience the taking on of subordinate roles as a 'free choice'. These sociologists have made important advances in our knowledge of the youth transition by revealing some of the processes which have ensured the smooth reproduction of class relations in capitalist society.

1.2 Youth and Class

A common assumption made by many of those who regarded the transition from school to work as smooth and orderly was that social class of origin, through its influence on educational outcomes, was a strong determinant of young people's objective life chances. Through their socialisation in the home and the school, young people developed assumptions about their place in the social world which reflected their positions in the social structure. Over the last two decades, changes in the structure and provision of education and training and changes in the labour market have led some to argue that the influence of class on life chances has declined and that we have now entered a new 'classless' society in which those with the appropriate talents and motivation can eventually overcome their initial handicaps. One of the main aims of this book is to examine whether the influence of class on young people's life chances has become any weaker: to discover whether young people growing up in John Major's 'classless society' really are able to break out of the cycles of inequality which constrained previous generations. In this study I found no evidence of a new meritocratic society, but before we consider the findings it is necessary to explore some of the assumptions which have been made about the relationship of young people to the system of stratification.

Despite the advances in our knowledge of the ways in which classes are reproduced which have come from work on the youth transition, many different assumptions are made about the position of youth in contemporary society. On the one hand, Feuer (1969) has described the generational struggle as the 'driving force of history', a force even more important than the class struggle. Marxists who follow this approach often regard the change in equilibrium between the material base and the ideological superstructure as being affected by youth as key agents of social change. Students at Kent State University in the 1960s and more recently in Tiananmen Square would be regarded as being in the front line of the broader class struggle. Thus youth is regarded as a separable concept which is central to the class struggle and to social dynamics (Mannheim, 1927; Feuer, 1969; Gillis, 1981). Mannheim (1927) made the distinction between generational consciousness and class consciousness. Generational consciousness can be seen as a youth-for-itself which, through its own distinctive culture, was overtly opposed to the dominant style of the adult generation and rebelled against it.

Among Marxists, such a view is controversial. Hall and Jefferson (1976), for example, regard it a 'unthinkable' to conceptualise youth as a class in its own right. They argue that youth subcultures 'continue to exist within, and co-exist with, the more inclusive culture of the class from which they spring', and 'membership of a subculture cannot protect them from the determining matrix of conditions and experiences which shape the life of their class as a whole' (Hall and Jefferson, 1976, pp. 14 and 15). Other sociologists have strongly rejected the argument that youth represents a class with its own interests which are opposed to adult interests. Parkin (1972), for example, recognised that young people are a disadvantaged group in so far as they are denied many of the privileges of adult society. For instance, they are paid low wages, not allowed to vote and not allowed to drink alcohol or marry without adult permission. In their day-to-day lives they are 'continually exposed to adult authority and domination, and very few areas of personal autonomy and independence are open to them' (Parkin, 1972 p. 16). However, Parkin rejects the notion that young people constitute a class because they are only youths for a limited period of time and because they are undergoing a process through which they will become incorporated into other classes. In other words, all they really share is their common experience of a transitory phase.

The youth transition is a crossroads in the process of social reproduction in that young people are at a stage where membership of their class of origin is about to be either confirmed or changed. The incorporation of youth into the socio-economic order is central to class dynamics, and the way in which incorporation takes place helps us to understand the way in which the existing social order is maintained. As such, young people should not be regarded as forming a separate class: their class position cannot be identified on an independent basis before they have entered the labour market and therefore occupy a position in relation to the means of production.

Even after they have entered their first jobs, there can be problems in accurately allocating young people to classes as many young people start work on the bottom rung of a career ladder. In these cases, on the basis of their first job they may be assigned to a lower class position to that which they are likely to achieve. Jones (1987) has tried to reconcile the transitory nature of youth with their position in the wider social structure, yet ultimately provides little more that a series of possible mobility routes.

Although Jones correctly identifies a potential source of error in the class analysis of young people, the career mobility of young people need not lead to a distorted class analysis so long as any classification takes account of the career structure (or lack of it), characteristic of different occupations. Ashton and Field's (1976) model is very simple yet does just this by classifying young people's jobs into one of three categories: 'careerless'; 'short-term career', and 'middle-class career'. This approach is justified as the career mobility of young workers tends to follow predictable patterns in which the likely progression of those in particular occupations can be easily identified; young people's first jobs have been found to be good predictors of their future life chances (Payne, 1987).

Changes in the nature of the transition have led to an additional dilemma in the interpretation of young people's class position, as their first experience in the labour market is now often as a 'trainee' rather than as an 'employee'. However, current research suggests that occupations in which young people are engaged whilst on schemes are a fairly reliable indicator of the level of occupation they are likely to enter after their schemes (Furlong and Raffe, 1989).

1.3 The changing transition

During the 1980s and 1990s the study of the transition from school to work became more complex as fewer young people were able to move directly from school to work. More young people entered post-compulsory education, and unemployment became a 'normal' part of young people's post-school experiences. With the decline in jobs for young people, and with the introduction and proliferation of work experience and training schemes, many young people now find that they are unable to get 'real' jobs until around two years after leaving school. Youth training schemes can delay the transition to stable employment and may introduce a higher degree of uncertainty into the process.

Because of the ways in which the transition to work has changed over the last decade, it is important to examine some of the key assumptions of the previous models of the transition from school to work. First of all it is important to question whether the process can still be conceptualised as relatively smooth. In other words, is it still true that young people's socialisation experiences in the home and the school prepare them for their subsequent experiences in the labour market, and is the transition still smooth owing to a tendency for their earlier expectations to be confirmed? I will suggest that for most young people the transition from school to work is still highly predictable: despite claims that we now live in a 'classless' society, family background still affects educational performance which in turn determines future labour market experiences.

In describing these changes in the transition from school to work, Roberts and colleagues (1986) make the distinction between the experiences of young people leaving school in the 1980s and typical experiences a decade earlier by calling the new transition the 'protracted transition'. However, while it is true that for most young people the transition to work is a more drawn-out process than was the case in the 1960s and 1970s, there are other important differences. In the 1980s and 1990s young people have followed a much wider variety of routes into the labour market than previously. Not only do they make the transition to work at different stages; they can fail to make a transition at different stages in their post-school careers and this can have a vital bearing on their future experiences.

The important question, however, is whether the existence of a greater variety of routes into the labour market results in more opportunities for young people to achieve upward social mobility. Do schemes represent a 'second opportunity' for those who leave school with few qualifications, or have they simply resulted in a 'two- stage' transition which produces 'double failures', as educational 'failures' become youth training 'failures' and either do not succeed in securing jobs, or find employment at the base of the occupational hierarchy?

In this book I re-examine the transition from school to work in order to find out whether the 'new' transition leads to greater opportunities for young people and whether the opportunity for work experience and training within a labour market context compensates for a lack of educational qualifications. Although it is often regarded as misleading to portray the transition from school to work as a simple 'trajectory' in which young people from different social backgrounds with different educational qualifications are 'propelled' to positions in the labour market, I will suggest that the structure of opportunities for young people has not changed radically over the last couple of decades. While there are certainly a greater variety of pathways which young people may follow from school to work, the system is no more open for most young people than previously: social class affects educational outcomes, and qualifications still have a powerful influence on labour market experiences.

Yet it is important to recognise that the crossroads at which social classes are reproduced and social inequalities reaffirmed has moved from the school gates into the labour market. As employers are brought into contact with young people for relatively long periods of time, they have been given the opportunity to rely on their own judgements as to the ability and acceptability of young people as workers rather than relying on evidence from schools and from short interviews. Although the process of social reproduction within the workplace may give an appearance of greater openness, which may in turn help to legitimise the structure of inequalities, for most young people school achievements remain good predictors of labour market outcomes as employers continue to select young people who have 'succeeded' at school.

1.4 The study

Most of the evidence on which the arguments presented in this book are based have been drawn from the Scottish Young People's Surveys (SYPS) which are described in detail in Appendix I. These are regular postal surveys which are carried out by the Centre for Educational Sociology at Edinburgh University. The SYPS currently comprises two overlapping 'arms': a leavers' survey which is sent to young people who left school in the previous academic year, and a cohort element which consists of young people who were in their fourth year of secondary schooling in the previous academic year. In Scotland, young people start secondary school a year later than in England so the Scottish fourth year is broadly equivalent to the English fifth year. It is the last year of compulsory schooling for those who reach the age of sixteen by 30 September following the year in which they started the fourth year. However, around a third of the year group will not have reached sixteen by this date and they have to remain at school until the following Christmas.

The leavers' survey has been carried out biennially since 1977; the cohort survey is a relatively recent addition which was developed in 1985 as a response to the changing nature of the transition from school to work. As youth unemployment rose and as young people came to spend much of the period after entering the labour market on schemes, the leavers' surveys (which only collected information up to a point ten months after the majority had left school) became inadequate to measure labour market experiences and outcomes. Much of the evidence in this book is derived from the '1985 cohort' of young people who had entered fourth year in September 1983 and who were first surveyed in spring 1985 (average age 16·75). The second survey of this cohort was carried out in spring 1986 (average age 17·75) and the third in autumn 1987 (average age 19·25).

Although there are many differences between the Scottish and
English education systems, most of the arguments presented in
this book are equally applicable to the transition from school to
work in England. The labour market in Scotland has undergone
similar changes to the English labour market and young people in
both countries have been forced to contend with the same training
schemes.

There are two main themes which integrate this book, which
have a bearing both on the ways in which we conceptualise the
transition, and on social policies directed towards young people.
The first theme is concerned with the effects of patterns of change
and continuity in the transition from school to work on structures
of class inequality in the 1990s. Essentially the book asks whether
the transition has become a more open process in which the
influence of social class of origin on young people's subsequent
life chances has become weaker. Previous models of the transition
from school to work portray a relatively smooth, linear process in
which social class of origin is one of the strongest determinants of
the trajectory young people follow through school and into unequal positions in the labour market. The evidence examined in
this book leads to the firm conclusion that young people still
follow highly stratified routes into the labour market and that
class inequalities show no evidence of decline.

While the Government has claimed to have created a classless
and meritocratic society, the policies it has pursued and the forms
of labour market intervention it has embarked on can be shown to
have reinforced existing class inequalities. The stratification of
youth training means that disadvantaged young people are
placed on the poorest schemes in unstable segments of the labour
market: few will find similar sorts of work on leaving their
schemes and their 'training' will largely have been a waste of
time. Indeed, many poorly qualified young people who enter
schemes will leave without jobs to go to, and as a consequence
will be labelled as 'double failures': they will then find themselves
trapped in a cycle of unemployment, subemployment, schemes
and 'shit jobs'.

The second theme which runs through the book is an attempt
to re-examine the ways in which young people experience the
transition from school to work and to challenge some of the
conventional wisdom which now surrounds it. In particular it is
argued that the transition is often an extremely difficult period in

young people's lives. On an objective level, the transition from school to work in the 1960s and 1970s might be regarded as having been a 'smooth' process as the pattern of movement between social class and position in the school and labour market were highly predictable. With the transition from school to work in the 1980s and 1990s being a more drawn-out process often involving experiences of unemployment and participation on schemes (which often do not carry any guarantee of a job), the 'new' transition may appear less predictable and therefore not as smooth. Bynner (1991), for example, has argued that there has been a breakdown in the mechanisms which previously ensured straightforward transitions. However, others have argued that it is wrong to portray the transition as a process which was once orderly, and that any model must incorporate 'disorder' (Rindfuss *et al.*, 1987).

On a subjective level, past sociological literature has often carried the assumption that our interpretation of events reflects 'objective' reality (e.g. Ashton and Field, 1976). This is not always the case. Because we, as sociologists, regard the social world in general, and the transition from school to work in particular, as highly structured and predictable, it does not mean that young people experience it in this way. The transition from school to work is a structured process which is experienced as 'free choice', but that is not to say that young people embrace the sorts of jobs they have been allocated. The cult of individual choice and meritocracy may eventually lead to an acceptance of one's fate in the labour market, but new entrants to the world of work often experience considerable frustration as they are forced to make downward adjustments to their occupational aspirations in the light of available opportunities.

In Chapter 2 I start to look for evidence of a more open opportunity structure by examining whether there has been any improvement in the position of pupils from less privileged backgrounds within the educational system. Despite changes in the organisation of education, it is argued that the relationship between family disadvantage and educational 'failure' remains strong. In Chapter 3 I examine aspects of change and continuity in the youth labour market over the decade 1977 to 1987 by looking at changes in post-school destinations and by analysing the effects of social class and educational achievement on young people's chances of obtaining 'respectable' jobs and on their chances of avoiding long-term unemployment. It is argued that despite many changes in the youth labour market over the past few years, there are many important continuities. Young people from privileged backgrounds and those with 'good' school qualifications continue to enjoy advantages in the labour market.

The introduction of work experience and training schemes for young people has had a radical effect on the nature of the transition from school to work over the last decade, and in Chapter 4 I look at the effects of schemes on the transition from school and weigh up some of the benefits and disadvantages associated with participation, both in terms of post-scheme experiences and in terms of young people's attitudes towards schemes. Despite evidence that scheme participation can give young people a small advantage in the labour market, it is argued that any advantages are outweighed by the high rate of post-scheme unemployment and by the difficulties many ex-trainees have in finding stable employment. Furthermore, the stratification of youth training and the fact that the best qualified school-leavers generally avoid schemes, means that this particular route into the labour market is unlikely to contribute towards the creation of a more open society.

Increasing levels of youth unemployment caused much concern in the late 1970s and early 1980s and were a major factor behind the introduction of schemes for young people, which were originally unemployment-based. In Chapter 5 I examine some of the reasons for the increase in unemployment, and at the social and psychological costs of unemployment. While young people's chances of unemployment are strongly affected by the overall levels of unemployment within the local labour market, it is argued that we can predict with a high degree of certainty which young people are most vulnerable to unemployment. Despite the greater protraction of the transition and the number of routes young people can follow between school and work, it is those who are socially or educationally disadvantaged who are most likely to experience unemployment.

Young people who have difficulties in finding regular employment may eventually decide to withdraw from the labour market rather than put up with the frustration of repeated rejection. In Chapter 6 I look at the characteristics of young people who withdraw from the labour market, the reasons why they withdraw, and examine the links between unemployment and labour market withdrawal. Young women with substantial experience of unemployment are most likely to regard labour market withdrawal as a means of escaping from the cycle of unemployment and schemes. However, I argue that unemployment is unlikely to erode young people's work ethics.

In any study of the transition from school it is important to develop an understanding of the subjective dimension of the transition alongside the objective dimension. In Chapter 7 I examine young people's occupational aspirations in order to discover more about their impressions about their future positions in the labour market. This allows us to judge whether subjective impressions match objective reality and to examine the extent to which young people are forced to make downward modifications to their aspirations. I argue that prior socialisation is not sufficiently strong to ensure that young people develop impressions about the occupational world which match reality, and that the transition from school to work tends to be a difficult period in young people's lives as they must frequently make downward modifications to their occupational aspirations. Moreover, I suggest that changes in the youth labour market are likely to have aggravated this situation.

Patterns of entry into the world of work are discussed in Chapter 8 and I analyse the ways in which educational attainments and post-16 experiences affect the sorts of jobs young people enter and discuss the effect of local labour market conditions on job entry. I argue that entry into the world of work has remained a highly structured process in which social and educational inequalities are reinforced. Although there are now a greater number of routes into the labour market, these remain highly stratified and there is little evidence to suggest that the greater diversity of routes has resulted in more equal opportunities. Indeed, it is argued that schemes often reinforce existing inequalities by placing disadvantaged young people in sectors of the labour market in which few will subsequently find employment.

In Chapter 9 I take a broader perspective on the transition by examining the ways in which transitional experiences are associated with different life styles among young adults and different patterns of leaving home. It is argued that those who are disadvantaged in occupational terms are unlikely to find compensation in other aspects of their social existence. To provide additional evidence of the effect of the transition on young people's subjective experiences, I conclude Chapter 9 by analysing the effects of post-16 experiences on young people's mental health I argue that common transitional experiences, such as becoming unemployed or entering situations which conflict with earlier expectations, can make the transition from school to work an extremely difficult period in young people's lives.

In the conclusion I argue that, despite numerous changes in the organisation of education and the youth labour market and the greater variety of routes young people will travel between school and work, there has been no real change in the structure of inequality. We have not entered a classless, meritocratic society, nor is there any discernible trend towards greater equality of opportunity. Furthermore, I suggest that for most young people, when we take account of both objective and subjective dimensions of the transition, it is clear that the transition from school to work is a difficult period in young people's lives.

Note

1. Springhall (1986) provides a good analysis and critique of the work of G. Stanley Hall.

2

EDUCATION, VOCATIONALISM AND INEQUALITY

2.1 Introduction

Over the last twenty years there have been a number of important
changes in the education system which may have affected young
people's experiences of the transition from school to work. Many
of these educational reforms have been implemented as a result
of concern over the 'wastage' of (working-class) talent in an
education system which has traditionally favoured pupils from
advantaged social backgrounds and concern about shortages of
qualified recruits for industry.

If the transition from school to work has changed over the last
couple of decades, if there are now more opportunities for young
people from working-class homes to enter jobs with reasonable
prospects and if Britain has indeed become a 'classless' society,
then we would expect to see an improvement in the position of
pupils from less advantaged backgrounds within the school. In
this chapter I examine whether the relative advantages of pupils
from different social backgrounds have changed: first by looking
at traditional qualifications and staying-on rates, and second by
assessing the contribution of the 'new vocationalism' to equality
of opportunity.

In capitalist societies, the unequal distribution of social and
economic rewards is often justified in terms of the opportunities
which people receive, and schools play an important role in
preparing young people for the positions they will enter in the
occupational hierarchy. As education is, in theory, available to
everyone, it has been suggested that 'one's position in the division
of labour could be portrayed as the result not of birth, but of one's
own efforts and talents' (Bowles, 1975, p. 261). In a society which
purports to be meritocratic, schools stand between family background and labour market position and are supposed to ensure that
the most able and best qualified people are placed in the best jobs.

Despite the common belief that ascribed occupational roles
have gradually been eroded, the truth of the matter is that social

ascent through education is limited, and family background has remained an important determinant of educational attainment throughout this century (Tyler, 1977; Reid, 1978; Halsey *et al.*, 1980; Gray *et al.*, 1983). A system of education which is available to all, regardless of social background or ability to pay, can legitimise inequalities by providing 'an open and ostensibly meritocratic mechanism for assigning individuals to unequal economic positions' (Sarup, 1982). Bourdieu describes this as the 'ideology of giftedness' which 'helps to enclose the underprivileged class in the roles which society has given them by making them see as natural inability things which are only the result of an inferior social status and by persuading them that they owe their social fate to their individual nature and their lack of gifts' (Bourdieu, 1974 p. 42).

Despite a facade of openness, the different education systems operating in the capitalist world[1] effectively guarantee success to a large proportion of the offspring of those occupying elite positions in the socio-economic order. For many years sociologists have tried to understand the mechanisms by which social class influences scholastic and occupational achievement in ways which do not lead to direct challenges to the legitimacy of the system. Much of the early work within the sociology of education focused upon the way in which the unequal distribution of resources in society affected educational performance and how social and economic disadvantage was translated into educational disadvantage.

At the beginning of the century, some of the more visible ways in which social background affected educational performance were used to explain the relationship. As Floud, Halsey and Martin (1957, p. 144) put it, 'poverty caused ill health and poor attendance, facilities for study could not be provided in slum houses, nor proper instruction given in overcrowded schools'. As educational facilities for working-class pupils improved and as absolute poverty declined, more refined theories were developed to explain the ways in which the social class of the parents influenced the future educational achievement of the child. Lower levels of remuneration for semi- and unskilled work were seen as resulting in a lack of resources to provide the stimulus necessary to give children the advantages enjoyed by their middle-class counterparts in the educational system. High levels of unemployment and employment instability within the lower working-class exacerbates this problem of lack of resources, which results in a primary concern being the problem of getting through each day rather than being able to plan for the future.

Social class also affects educational performance in other, less obvious, ways. Bernstein (1971), for example, suggested that the acquisition of different lingual codes by children from different social class backgrounds affects the schools' view of the ability of the child. In a similar vein, Bourdieu (1973, 1974) has argued that middle-class advantages in the educational system are largely due to the similarity between middle-class culture and the dominant culture and that the mode of learning employed in schools is similar to that practised within middle-class families: 'Teachers assume that they already share a common language and set of values with their pupils', but the lower classes 'only acquire with great effort something which is given to the children of the cultivated classes' (Bourdieu, 1974, p. 39).

In the 1950s and 1960s a predominance of functionalist perspectives in sociology meant that the desirability of educational success was often taken for granted. More recently, the processes whereby the cultural manifestations of social class can predetermine educational outcomes has been explored in the ethnographic literature. Willis (1977) and Jenkins (1983), for example, argued that the normative orientations of the young people themselves are of prime importance in determining educational success. The generally poor academic performance of young people from lower working-class backgrounds can be seen as a consequence of their rejection of 'success' in middle-class terms.

Working-class 'life styles' often emphasise different sets of values and priorities than middle-class styles of life (Jenkins, 1983; Willis, 1977). It has been argued in this context that working-class action is present orientated and linked to impulse gratification, whilst middle-class action is more likely to be future orientated and based upon deferred gratification. As such, there tends to be a conflict between academic success, which requires a postponement of immediate rewards in order to gain future advantages, and working-class values which stress the importance of enjoyment in the here and now (Ashton and Field, 1976). However, other evidence suggests that the relationship between school attitude and social class is weak (Ashton *et al.*, 1986; Furlong, 1988a). Furthermore, while young people from lower working-class families may reject a school culture which is based on

predominantly middle-class values, the school places a high pre-
mium on middle-class cultural attributes such as forms of language, dress and demeanour. Without the necessary characteristics a working-class pupil can be at a disadvantage despite a
desire to succeed at school.

Many of the classic British works on the relationship between
social class and educational achievement were conducted prior to
the introduction of Comprehensive education, which was introduced as a means of providing the conditions under which young
people would have greater equality of opportunity through being
educated in a common school, irrespective of ability. In theory,
Comprehensive schools were supposed to encourage a greater
social mix of pupils, which in turn would aid the academic performance of lower-class pupils. Early research into the effects of
Comprehensive schooling suggested that these goals were not
being met. Ford (1969), for example, found that Comprehensives
did not lead to a greater social mix within peer groups. This
failure was largely blamed on the continued use of ability streams
within Comprehensive schools which reinforced the effects of
social class. Ford (1969) argued that the middle-class child stood a
better chance of placement in the upper streams than did the
working-class child. Similarly, Ball (1981) has suggested that
banding in Comprehensive schools has resulted in a system
which is no fairer in terms of equality of opportunity than the bi-
partite system which it replaced.

Ford undertook her study during the early stages of
Comprehensivisation and Ball focused on just one school. Recent
evidence from the Scottish Young People's Surveys has been
more encouraging. McPherson and Willms (1987) have argued
that, in Scotland, Comprehensive schools have had a positive
effect on standards of attainment of young people from working-
class families. Between 1976 and 1984 a process of 'equalisation'
took place as pupils with a socio-economic status (SES) one standard deviation below the national average increased their attainment relative to pupils of average SES. This improvement in
performance was in the region of one O grade pass for males and
half an O grade pass for females. However, this trend did not
extend to the upper levels of attainment or to the post-compulsory stages of secondary schooling. Moreover, the Scottish Education Department has tended to show a greater commitment to the
principles of Comprehensive education than many of the English

Local Education Authorities (Gray *et al.*, 1983): therefore we cannot assume that the effects of Comprehensivisation in England are comparable.

2.2 Trends in educational outcomes

Despite any improvement in the qualifications of working-class pupils which may have been brought about through Comprehensive education, there is still a strong relationship between social class and school qualifications throughout Britain. In Scotland over the decade 1977 to 1987 there was a distinct trend towards better qualifications among pupils from all social classes, yet the relationship between class[2] and qualifications is striking (Table 2.1). In 1987, for example, about four in ten young people from the lower working-class (Registrar General's Classes IV and V) (45 per cent of males and 39 per cent of females) left school with no O grade passes compared with around one in ten young people (13 per cent of males and 10 per cent of females) from the professional and managerial class (Registrar General's Classes I and II). At the other end of the scale, nearly half of the females (49 per cent) and over four in ten males (44 per cent) from the professional and managerial class gained the three Highers which would, in theory, give them access to higher education. In contrast, only about one in ten young people from the lower working-class (10 per cent of males and 9 per cent of females) had three or more Highers.

In a study of the relationship between school attainment and entry to higher education between 1976 and 1986 among Scottish school-leavers, Burnhill and colleagues (1988) attempted to predict the relative chances of young people from different class backgrounds gaining the qualifications which would allow them to seek entry to higher education. Using a multivariate model, they predicted that the relative chances of a young person with a father in social class I gaining three or more Highers was nearly six times greater than for a young person with a father in a manual occupation. They also demonstrated the existence of a strong relationship between parental education and gaining three or more Highers. When both parents had been educated to at least the age of 17, the child's relative chances of gaining three or more Highers was around four-and-a-half times greater than if both parents had finished their education at or before the age of 15. However, the evidence presented by Burnhill and colleagues

TABLE 2.1 Total SCEs on leaving school by class and sex: 1977–1987 (%)

		1977	1979	1981	1983	1985	1987
Professional & Managerial Class							
No O Grade at A-C	Male	15	10	13	14	11	13
	Female	14	14	10	12	11	10
1-4 O Grades	Male	20	22	21	20	20	19
	Female	20	19	17	15	15	17
5+ O Grades	Male	8	12	10	9	9	10
	Female	7	10	11	10	6	7
1-2 Highers	Male	17	14	12	14	14	14
	Female	18	16	17	17	19	16
3+ Highers	Male	39	41	43	43	47	44
	Female	41	41	45	46	49	49
Unweighted n	Male	(410)	(672)	(676)	(840)	(794)	(721)
	Female	(432)	(705)	(707)	(789)	(737)	(830)
Upper Working Class							
No O Grades at A-C	Male	46	41	42	40	36	37
	Female	46	40	38	36	28	28
1-4 O Grades	Male	26	30	29	29	28	30
	Female	27	29	29	28	29	31
5+ O Grades	Male	8	9	8	8	10	9
	Female	6	8	8	7	9	9
1-2 Highers	Male	7	7	8	9	10	10
	Female	8	9	11	13	15	14
3+ Highers	Male	13	12	13	14	16	13
	Female	12	13	14	17	19	17
Unweighted n	Male	(951)	(1223)	(1154)	(1639)	(1182)	(1083)
	Female	(932)	(1276)	(1236)	(1524)	(1257)	(1134)
Lower Working Class							
No O Grades at A-C	Male	57	57	55	50	46	45
	Female	54	53	54	46	38	39
1-4 O Grades	Male	24	25	25	27	27	32
	Female	25	26	24	28	29	29
5+ O Grades	Male	5	8	7	7	8	7
	Female	5	6	7	5	7	7
1-2 Highers	Male	5	4	6	8	8	7
	Female	7	7	6	10	11	14
3+ Highers	Male	9	7	7	8	11	10
	Female	8	8	8	10	15	9
Unweighted n	Male	(337)	(503)	(474)	(540)	(488)	(380)
	Female	(403)	(570)	(524)	(565)	(495)	(431)

indicated that there had been no change between 1976 and 1986 in the effect of either parental education or social class on the chances of gaining three or more Highers.

The relationship between class-based inequalities and educational attainment in Britain remains strong, and despite any improvement brought about by Comprehensive education (which although significant are nevertheless small), attainment is still strongly determined by social class and this has changed little since the war (Halsey *et al.*, 1980; Gray *et al.*, 1983). While strong differences in levels of educational attainment among young people from different social classes have persisted, gender-based inequalities in school attainment have been greatly reduced during the last decade. In the 1960s and 1970s, boys tended to outperform girls throughout secondary schooling (Douglas, 1967). More boys sat and passed O grades and O levels and more sat and passed Highers and A levels. Since the mid-1970s, girls started to catch up with the boys in terms of secondary school performance, and by the early 1980s were outperforming the boys at school. Furthermore, girls were starting to outperform the boys in subjects which previously favoured boys, such as arithmetic (Willms and Kerr, 1987).

2.3 Trends in educational participation

Despite slow improvements in the relative educational performance of working-class pupils over the last decade, there has been an important trend towards greater levels of participation in post-compulsory education among all social classes. In Scotland, between 1977 and 1987 the proportion of pupils leaving school at the end of the fourth year declined from 62 per cent to 43 per cent for males and from 59 per cent to 43 per cent for females (Table 2.2). The proportion who left school from the fifth year increased from 21 per cent and 27 per cent for males and females respectively in 1977, to 35 per cent and 38 per cent in 1987. The proportion leaving school from the sixth year increased from 16 per cent and 14 per cent for males and females respectively in 1977, to 22 per cent and 24 per cent in 1987.

In England, up until the early 1970s, most young people left school at the minimum age and only those with 'good' qualifications were given any encouragement to start a post- compulsory year (Roberts *et al.*, 1989). Roberts and colleagues have shown that throughout the 1980s nearly half of all 16-year-olds remained in

table 2.2 Stage of leaving school by sex, and proportion of minimum-age school-leavers by social class: 1977-1987

	1977 Male	1977 Female	1979 Male	1979 Female	1981 Male	1981 Female	1983 Male	1983 Female	1985 Male	1985 Female	1987 Male	1987 Female
% leaving school at end of fourth year	62	59	61	59	57	52	45	41	46	39	43	38
% leaving school from fifth year	21	27	22	26	25	31	34	36	32	37	35	38
% leaving school from sixth year	16	14	16	14	17	18	20	23	21	24	22	24
Unweighted n	(1923)	(2017)	(2882)	(3066)	(2666)	(2882)	(3597)	(3450)	(3167)	(3172)	(3752)	(2999)

Social Class	1977 I+II	1977 IIIn IIIm	1977 IV +V	1979 I+II	1979 IIIn IIIm	1979 IV +V	1981 I+II	1981 IIIn IIIm	1981 IV +V	1983 I+II	1983 IIIn IIIm	1983 IV +V	1985 I+II	1985 IIIn IIIm	1985 IV +V	1987 I+II	1987 IIIn IIIm	1987 IV +V
% leaving school at minimum age	34	71	77	35	72	82	27	68	78	26	59	70	25	57	65	22	44	48
Unweighted n base	(843)	(1884)	(740)	(1337)	(2499)	(1073)	(1383)	(2390)	(998)	(1632)	(3174)	(1118)	(1535)	(2442)	(990)	(1557)	(2230)	(822)

Note: 1. 1977 figures are based on four regions (Strathclyde, Lothian, Fife and Tayside).
2. Class I and II professional and managerial, IIIn & IIIm upper working class, IV & V lower working class.

full-time education, although only around half of these were in the 'academic mainstream' leading to qualifications for entry into higher education.

In Scotland the picture was more complex because changing school entry regulations resulted in a lower proportion of young people being eligible to leave school at the end of the fourth year (Burnhill, 1984). These young people, known as the 'conscripts', increased from 17 per cent of the year group in 1978 to 27 per cent in 1983 (Tomes, 1988a). The increasing numbers of 'conscripts' in each school year only explains part of the decrease in fourth year leavers in Scotland which, between 1977 and 1984, fell from 54 per cent to 36 per cent for females and from 56 per cent to 43 per cent for boys (Tomes, 1988a). As in England, the proportion of young people who entered post-compulsory education rose partly as a result of increasing youth unemployment and partly due to changes in the social composition of the school year groups whereby a greater proportion came from non-manual social classes and more had parents who had experienced post-compulsory education themselves (Burnhill, 1984; Tomes, 1988a). As young people started to experience difficulties in finding work after school and as Government-sponsored work experience and training schemes started to replace jobs for minimum-age school-leavers, more young people in Scotland started to opt for post-compulsory education in preference to taking their chances in the labour market. This trend was not so apparent in England where the two-year A level course demands a greater commitment than the one-year Highers course.

Raffe and Willms (1989) have argued that, because there is a strong relationship between levels of unemployment in an area and participation in post-compulsory education, young people are more likely to stay on at school in areas with high rates of unemployment. Again, there is no evidence of a comparable effect in England. In Scotland, this 'discouraged worker' effect was found to be strongest for young people with average to above-average levels of attainment who may have been undecided as to whether to stay-on or to leave. The effect was similar for males and females. However, as young people in high unemployment areas tended to have lower school attainment than those in lower unemployment areas, the effect of unemployment on staying-on rates was partly offset (Raffe and Willms, 1989).

Over the decade there has been both an increase in the

TABLE 2.3 'Why did you start a fifth year?', by sex and social class

	1981 Male	1981 Female	1987 Male	1987 Female	1981 I+II	1981 IIIn+IIIm	1981 IV+V	1987 I+II	1987 IIIn+IIIm	1987 IV+V
I was too young to leave at the end of fourth year	27	26	45	42	22	29	32	31	47	53
There were no jobs available that I wanted	14	11	16	15	7	17	17	12	17	19
I enjoyed school life	30	42	25	36	38	36	35	37	27	26
I was too young to enter the job or course I'd chosen	10	16	8	12	14	13	12	10	11	8
I hadn't decided on my future education or career	47	45	39	41	50	45	42	49	37	35
I'd always assumed I would start a fifth year	52	58	44	50	67	48	43	65	41	35
Unweighted n	(1185)	(1431)	(1564)	(1861)	(1060)	(989)	(310)	(1213)	(1236)	(423)

Notes: 1. Totals exceed 100 as respondends could tick more than one box.
2. Only the six items reported here were used in both years. However, additional items were included in both years.
3. Class I + II professional and managerial, IIIn + IIIm upper working class, IV + V lower working class.

proportion of pupils who have parents who themselves experienced post-compulsory education, as well as an increase in the proportion of young people with fathers in non-manual occupations (Burnhill *et al.*, 1988). These changes in the social composition of the school year group have also been an important factor in leading to greater levels of post-compulsory education among young people: those whose parents had experienced post-compulsory education and those whose fathers worked in non-manual occupations were more likely to stay on at school.

Young people whose parents entered post-compulsory education were more than twice as likely to stay on for a post-compulsory year than were those whose parents were minimum-age school-leavers. Young people with fathers in white-collar occupations were more than twice as likely to enter post-compulsory education than those with fathers working in manual occupations (Burnhill, 1984). Parental encouragement to remain in education varies with social class. One of the reasons for this trend is that young people from middle-class homes and those whose parents had experienced extended education were more likely to receive encouragement to remain at school from parents who were aware of the potential benefits (Jackson and Marsden, 1962; Douglas, 1967; Plowden Report, 1967; Furlong, 1988a).

Nevertheless, over the decade 1977 to 1987, the decrease in the proportion of young people who left school at the minimum age (fourth-year leavers and those leaving at Christmas of the fifth year) was not as great among those with fathers in the professional and managerial class as it was among those from other social classes. Over this decade, the proportion of minimum-age school-leavers from the upper working-class (Registrar General's Classes IIIn and IIIm) decreased by 27 per cent and by 29 per cent among those from the lower working-class (Registrar General's Classes IV and V); yet in the professional and managerial class the fall was around 12 per cent. However, despite these trends towards equalisation, in 1987 the proportion of minimum-age school-leavers in both the upper and lower working-classes was still more than double that among those from the professional and managerial class (Table 2.2).

In both 1981 and 1987 respondents to the SYPS were asked to give their reasons for starting a fifth year at school (Table 2.3). In 1987, more than four in ten young people said that they started a fifth year because they were too young to leave at the end of the fourth year. In 1981, fewer than three in ten gave this as a reason. This trend reflects the increase in the proportion of 'conscripts' in the school year group. For many young people in Scotland, there is no real decision to be made at the end of fourth year about whether to stay on as many young people had always assumed that they would start a fifth year. However, fewer young people made this assumption in 1987 than in 1981 which perhaps reflects the greater range of post-16 options which had become available as well as a greater uncertainty in the youth labour market. This attitude was stronger among females than males and was particularly strong among young people from higher social classes. Nearly two-thirds (65 per cent) of those with fathers in the professional and managerial class said that they had always assumed they would start a fifth year, as compared with just over a third (35 per cent) of those with fathers in the lower working-classes.

In Britain, there is a sense in which post-16 education is part of the assumptive world of the middle-classes and a majority of working-class pupils never consider remaining in education after sixteen (Furlong, 1988a). Thus while the decision to remain in education is experienced as a free choice, it is heavily structured and influenced by the taken-for-granted assumptions in a particular society or social class. In contrast to Britain, Ashton (1988) suggests that in Canada there is a generalised assumption that a young person will remain at school until they are eighteen.

The relationship between social class and the decision to leave school is fairly complex and goes beyond taken-for-granted assumptions. Levels of parental encouragement are influenced by their child's school achievements, as well as by the sorts of occupations available in the local labour market and the qualifications required to enter them. Those who remain in education in preference to entering the labour market often do so in the belief that such a strategy will pay off in terms of their future career (Furlong, 1988a). Indeed, a young person's decision about whether to leave education at the minimum age appears to be influenced by the structure of the local labour market they grow up in. Coles (1986) has suggested that these 'area factors' are important as a young person's willingness to stay on at school and get higher qualifications are dependent upon the opportunities available in the local labour market. One of the reasons why young people in Canada are more willing to remain at school until eighteen than are young people in Britain is that employers' recruitment policies are not focused towards 16-year-old leavers the way they are in Britain (Ashton, 1988).

Another important reason given by young people for starting a fifth year at school was that they hadn't decided on their future careers. However, in 1987 fewer young people were giving this as a reason for staying on at school than in 1981. The reason for this is unclear: it may be that the decline in opportunities in the youth labour market made young people sharpen their thinking at an earlier age, or perhaps made them more willing to accept any job. On the other hand, the existence of training schemes and the proliferation of vocational courses may have provided alternatives for those who were unsure about their future careers. More predictably, the proportion of young people who started a fifth year at school because of a lack of certain sorts of jobs increased between 1981 and 1987, yet this increase was relatively small: for males it increased by 2 percentage points, while for females it increased by 4 percentage points.

As we have seen, part of the increase in post-compulsory schooling in Scotland has been a result of changes affecting school entry which has led to an increase in the proportion of the year group who are unable to leave school until Christmas of the fifth year. Having been made to complete the longest term of the academic year (in Scotland the autumn term starts in August) young people may be encouraged to complete the school year, especially if they regard Highers as being within their reach. Yet completing fifth year is not necessarily beneficial to those outside of the academic mainstream (who completed fifth year without studying or sitting Highers) as they often gain few additional SCEs. Until recently, those 'conscripts' who intended to leave school at Christmas often did not start any new courses and few gained any additional qualifications as a result of their extra term at school. Among the 1985 fourth year cohort, 'conscripts' gained an average of 1·2 O grades during fifth year (although some will have gained other qualifications such as Scotvec modules).

2.4 Vocational education

With respect to 'traditional' qualifications and patterns of participation in post-compulsory education, any discernible trend towards a more open, meritocratic system of education could be described as being largely superficial. Yet perhaps the most radical change in education in recent years has been the growth of vocationalism in schools. Given these attempts to provide greater freedom of access to rewarding positions in the labour market, one cannot dismiss the efforts of educationalists to provide greater equality of opportunity without considering the impact of these changes.

In 1984 an attempt was made to rationalise existing qualifications and to provide a new, integrated approach to non-advanced vocational education with the introduction of the Scottish Action Plan (SED, 1983). This system was based on a modular approach (consisting of notional 40-hour certificated modules) in which students could tailor programmes to their own particular needs and circumstances. The system was to be flexible so that young people could build a programme around the courses on offer in different settings such as at school, on YTS and at further education colleges, as well as being able to combine full-time and part-time modes of study. It was argued that a flexible, modular approach to vocational education would allow the curriculum to be responsive to the changing needs of individuals and industry (Lowden, 1989). It was intended that the flexibility of modules would help motivate young people to put themselves forward for training by encouraging them to 'collect' modules. Raffe (1988a) describes the ways in which the possession of some modules provides young people with the incentive to gain more modules through being seen as 'Lego starter sets'. The possession of an introductory set enhances the value of any further sets which are bought and provides extra incentives.

If the modular system is supposed to motivate young people to build on and consolidate courses of modules, then it is important that they react favourably to these courses. Initial evidence suggests that young people's overall attitudes towards modules were positive. Lowden (1989) has shown that students tended to regard the courses as well taught and interesting. In addition, they felt that the modular courses fitted together well to provide a good overall course. However, despite these positive features, the Action Plan seems to be providing vocational education for working-class and less qualified young people, particularly within the schools. Young people who were taking modules in the fifth year at school tended to be the lower qualified, and modular courses were used extensively as short courses for the 'conscripts' who had started a fifth year because they were too young to have left school at the end of the fourth year (Tomes, 1988a). However, among YTS trainees it was the better qualified young people who were most likely to have taken modules.

What has become known as the 'new vocationalism' is apparent in the Scottish Action Plan but is perhaps most visible in the Technical and Vocational Education Initiative (TVEI). TVEI was introduced as a pilot scheme in England in 1983, and extended to Scotland a year later in 1984. The main aim of TVEI was to encourage the development of 'broadly based occupational skills and competencies' in school pupils between the ages of 14 and 18 in order to give them a 'relevant and practical preparation for adult and working life' (Bell *et al.*, 1988). In practical terms, young people in Scotland who started TVEI in 1984 while in the third year often spent as little as one afternoon per week on TVEI work. The TVEI programme consisted of core and optional courses. Core courses included information technology, personal and social development, careers and work experience. Optional courses often included subjects such as computing, catering, business studies and control technology (Bell *et al.*, 1988).

In their evaluation of the pilot TVEI programmes in Scotland, Bell and colleagues (1988) argued that TVEI was blurring the boundaries between school and employment by making the curriculum more relevant to industry and commerce, helping young people to understand the world of commerce and industry, and thus easing young people's transition from school to work. To this extent, TVEI seems to have been successful in achieving the aims set down for it. However, while the scheme is aimed at all young people, irrespective of sex or ability, in practice the first intake was biased towards males and pupils of lower ability. Of those members of the year group who did not join TVEI, 33 per cent achieved no O grade passes, this compared to 45 per cent of TVEI students. Of the young people on TVEI, 58 per cent were male and 42 per cent were female (Bell *et al.*, 1988).

This bias towards males and low-achievers has led to accusations that TVEI is the 'vocationalisation of working-class education' (Brown, 1987a), and that the hidden cost of the initiative may be an increase in class and gender inequalities (Brown, 1987a; Blackman, 1987). Indeed, Brown argues that TVEI is a policy which 'attempts to legitimate the provision of a socially appropriate training, rather than a socially "just" education for large numbers of working-class pupils' (1987b, p. 128). Brown identifies the use of pupil 'profiles' on TVEI as a mechanism by which teachers can ensure the compliance of their pupils. With the use of 'profiles', young people's personalities are treated as packages which must be traded in the market place and it becomes necessary for young people to conform in order to make sure that their 'profile' will help them in the search for work (Brown, 1987b). Despite massive investment in TVEI, there is no evidence, as yet, that the initiative is having positive measurable results. Raffe (1989a) examined the first TVEI cohort in terms of four criteria: examination attainment at sixteen; truancy; continuing full-time education after sixteen; and employment among those who leave. On only one of these performance indicators, truancy, did TVEI have a statistically significant favourable effect.

Young people who truant tend to be those who are taking few examinations, those from lower social classes, those from large families and from families with no adult male. Nevertheless, a majority of young people reported truanting at some time during their fourth year at school (Gray *et al.*, 1983). In 1977, nearly seven in ten males (68 per cent) and nearly six in ten females (59 per cent) reported having truanted at some time during their fourth year at school. By 1983 this had declined to 59 per cent of males and 51 per cent of females, but then increased to 62 per cent and 53 per cent of males and females respectively by 1987. The fall in truancy in Scotland between 1977 and 1983 has been explained by Raffe (1986a) as being partly a result of increasing levels of youth unemployment as the fall in levels of truancy coincided with the period in which youth unemployment rates rose sharply. Raffe argued that high levels of unemployment within a labour market reduces truancy by increasing pupil motivation. Other factors which may have been responsible for declining truancy rates include the increasing perceived relevance of the school curriculum to working life brought about by more use of vocational education, as well as the element of coercion implicit in the use of character assessment and profiles.

Given that policy-makers regard TVEI as a means by which the curriculum can be made more relevant to the world of work, and because an increased relevance may give it legitimacy in the eyes of working-class pupils who previously tended to regard school work as irrelevant to their future needs (Ashton and Field, 1976; Brown, 1987b), it is worth looking in detail at young people's perceptions of TVEI. Among the TVEI students in the Scottish evaluation, many believed that the initiative had changed teaching and learning methods for the better, and regarded it as having had a positive effect on their motivation and achievement. In comparison to non-TVEI pupils, those who were on TVEI were more likely to say that they learnt a lot about how to apply for jobs, about how to handle job interviews, about jobs which they might like to do and the sorts of jobs available in the area, and about what it is like to be at work and how to set up their own businesses (Bell *et al.*, 1988). However, Bell and colleagues argued that, despite these benefits, pupils tended to feel that a problem with TVEI was the low status granted to vocational education. In other words, the initiative was popular because it was perceived as more relevant to their future needs than the traditional curriculum. Yet however relevant these qualifications are to industrialists or pupils, we cannot seriously expect courses which are widely regarded in the schools as suitable only for the less able to have a real impact on young people's life chances.

2.5 Conclusion

Despite the 'new vocationalism' apparent in initiatives like TVEI, and curricular innovations like Action Plan, vocationalism appears to have done little to reduce class- and gender-based inequalities in educational achievement. Although designed to have a broad appeal, both TVEI and Action Plan (at least in the schools) have so far failed to appeal to a wide range of pupils. While Comprehensive schools do seem to have led to some improvement in the performance of working-class pupils, the advances made to date are not great and do not extend to the higher levels of achievement.

Although a lack of resources in the home and in schools in poor neighbourhoods continue to inhibit the educational development of many pupils, there is a lack of consensus on the relative influence on educational attainment of material deprivation and normative orientations or cultural capital. The view that working-class pupils do not regard educational success as important has been heavily contested (Brown, 1987b), yet the belief in the existence of differential value systems is implicit in much of the thinking behind the 'new vocationalism'.

Vocationalism has largely been aimed at those who are assumed to regard traditional education as irrelevant to their future needs in the labour market. Those who oppose the spread of vocational education often do so on the grounds that it creates a two-tier education system and because of the strong empirical evidence that, despite what they say, when it comes to recruitment employers undervalue vocational qualifications in comparison with traditional educational qualifications. While both of these reasons are valid ones, it is nevertheless important to look at the content of the curriculum from the point of view of the young people themselves if they are to be encouraged to remain at school beyond the minimum age.

Even among those young people who 'succeed' at school, many find their lessons boring and regard their schooling as a waste of time. They may put in the work at school, but they regard school instrumentally as a means of getting a 'reasonable' job (Brown, 1987b). If young people are to gain from their schooling, then it is important for them to leave with more than a handful of 'pieces of paper'. There is little point in forcing disaffected pupils to continue with a curriculum they have rejected. Yet two-tier education is unfair because one of the tracks will inevitably be regarded as inferior and will lead to disadvantaged positions within the labour market as employers will discriminate in favour of those seen as holding the superior qualification. Perhaps the only real solution is the abolition of the traditional SCE and GCSE qualifications which do more to create failures and maintain class differentials than to encourage academic excellence. A move towards a general high school leaving diploma awarded to all pupils attaining set levels of competence in their chosen subjects would be a move in the right direction.

Notes

1. Although the education systems in Britain and America are organised differently (the American system characterised by contest mobility, the British by sponsored mobility), Kerckhoff (1990) has argued that both systems produce similar levels of social mobility.
2. In this book, class analysis is based on the Registrar General's social classes using father's current or most recent occupation. In many respects the Registrar General's social classes are inadequate and use of the male occupation can obscure important differences within families. However, details of mothers' occupations were not collected by the SYPS for all the survey years included in this analysis. Moreover, there are certain difficulties associated with asking young people to provide details of their mother's 'best' occupations or the occupations they trained in.

3

CHANGE AND CONTINUITY
IN THE YOUTH TRANSITION

3.1 Introduction

In many parts of Britain, in the 1960s and early 1970s, young people tended to make fairly direct transitions from school to work, occasionally interrupted by a short spell of unemployment. This was certainly the case for those young people, often from working-class families, who had few educational qualifications (Ashton and Field, 1976). Young people with more qualifications often made their transition by way of an extended period of post-16 education or training. This sometimes took the form of a short vocational course at college and sometimes took the form of a longer transitional pattern including a period of post-compulsory schooling and higher education before starting work.

By the early 1980s this description of the transition from school to work had become outdated. Young people were tending to build up a much greater range of experiences between the end of compulsory schooling and starting work. This new extended transition was termed the 'protracted' transition (Roberts *et al.*, 1986) or the 'broken transition' (Griffin, 1986) and sociologists who attempted to describe this increasingly complex transition tended to identify large numbers of overlapping routes which young people were following into the labour market (Clough *et al.*, 1986; Furlong and Raffe, 1989).

The increase in the complexity of the transition from school to work was largely a result of changes which were taking place in the youth labour market. During the 1970s levels of school-leaver unemployment rose and the proportion of young people entering full-time employment on leaving school steadily declined. This trend became particularly severe after 1979 (Raffe, 1983a). Because of the decline in youth jobs, fewer young people were able to move directly from school to work and a majority of minimum-age school-leavers came to experience Government-sponsored work experience and training schemes or unemployment.

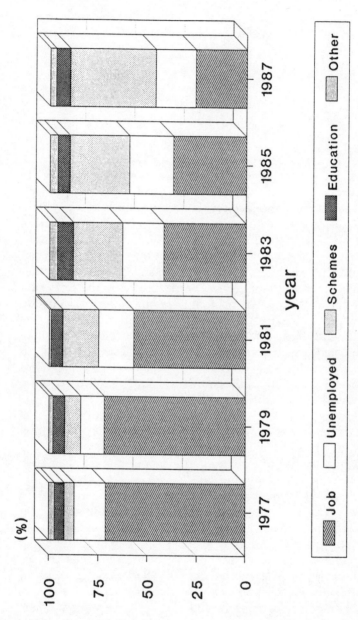

FIGURE 3.1 Spring destinations of minimum age school-leavers (%).
1977 figures are based on four regions, Strathclyde, Lothian, Fife and Tayside.

In the previous chapter, I suggested that one of the responses to the collapse in the youth labour market was a fall in the proportion of young people (especially females) who entered the labour market at the minimum age.[1] Of those who started their fourth year of secondary schooling in 1983, one in two (44 per cent of males and 56 per cent of females) followed routes into the labour market which included either schooling after fourth year or full-time further education, and nearly one in five (19 per cent) entered full-time further education (14 per cent of males and 24 per cent of females) (Furlong and Raffe, 1989). Young people with above-average qualifications were particularly likely to have followed routes into the labour market which included participation in post-compulsory education. For those with few educational attainments, the possibility of further education was less attractive and they tended to enter the labour market at an earlier stage than their better qualified peers (Furlong and Raffe, 1989). Yet among those who entered the labour market, the loss of youth jobs and the experience of unemployment has disproportionately affected unqualified young people (Ashton *et al.*, 1982; Raffe, 1983b; Furlong and Raffe, 1989). Those who left school without qualifications found it particularly difficult to find jobs, and the early work experience schemes such as the Job Creation Programme (JCP) and the Youth Opportunities Programme (YOP) mainly recruited unqualified young people (Raffe, 1984b). Attempts were made to attract more qualified school-leavers on to schemes with the introduction of the Youth Training Scheme (YTS), yet the composition of schemes continued to be skewed towards lower-qualified young people (Raffe, 1988b; Furlong and Raffe, 1989).

In this chapter I concentrate on minimum-age school-leavers (as it is this group who have been most affected by the changes in the youth labour market),[2] and examine some of the ways in which they have experienced the decline in the youth labour market over the decade 1977 to 1987. Although the typical post-school experiences of school-leavers in 1987 are quite different from the typical experiences in 1977, there are still important similarities. The youth labour market in 1987 is similar to that of 1977 insofar as those who are advantaged in terms of social background or education still tend to enter the most desirable jobs and schemes and rarely experience prolonged unemployment.

TABLE 3.1 Spring destinations of minimum-age school-leavers: 1977-1987 (%)

		1977+	1979	1981	1983	1985	1987
Schemes	Male	7	9	19	24	34	46
	Female	3	7	17	25	26	40
Full-time job	Male	74	76	61	48	37	27
	Female	70	68	52	35	36	24
Unemployed	Male	16	12	18	21	23	21
	Female	15	12	18	20	22	19
Full-time	Male	1	2	2	3	3	3
Education	Female	8	10	11	14	10	12
Other	Male	2	1	*	3	3	2
	Female	4	2	1	5	6	5
Unweighted n	Male	(1160)	(1852)	(1575)	(2007)	(1683)	(1068)
	Female	(1144)	(1904)	(1538)	(1683)	(1427)	(1042)
Total	Male	100	100	100	99	100	99
	Female	100	99	99	99	100	100

Notes: 1. + 1977 figures are based on four regions (Strathclyde, Lothian, Fife and Tayside). Other years are Scotland-wide.
2. * less than 0.5 per cent.
3. Destinations are self reported, unemployment is defined as 'unemployed and looking for work'.

3.2 Changes in the transition

In the spring of 1977, more than seven in ten 1976 minimum-age school-leavers in Scotland (74 per cent of males and 70 per cent of females) were in full-time employment. In contrast, in the spring of 1987, fewer than three in ten 1986 school-leavers (27 per cent of males and 24 per cent of females) were working full-time (Table 3.1). Certainly the most dramatic of the changes in the Scottish youth labour market over the decade 1977 to 1987 was this sharp decline in the proportion of leavers entering full-time employment (Figure 3.1). In 1977 most minimum-age school-leavers had entered full-time jobs by the spring after leaving school. By 1987 it was a minority who were working in the spring after leaving school.

The collapse in the youth labour market in Scotland was was only partly reflected in the unemployment figures. Spring unemployment among minimum-age school-leavers reached a peak in 1985, and by that time had risen by around 7 percentage points since 1977 (from 16 per cent to 23 per cent for males and from 15 per cent to 22 per cent for females). The discrepancy between the steep fall in jobs and the less severe rise in unemployment was mainly accounted for by the growth of work experience and training schemes as well as a (smaller) increase in participation in post-school education. Between 1977 and 1987 scheme participation grew by a staggering 38 percentage points (from 7 per cent of male and 3 per cent of female minimum-age leavers in 1977 to 46 per cent of males and 40 per cent of females in in 1987).[3]

These changes in the youth labour market did not affect all young people in the same way. Qualified school-leavers continued to have different post-school experiences from unqualified leavers, and those from privileged social backgrounds continued to experience the transition differently to those from less privileged backgrounds. Although there were differences in the typical post-school destinations of males and females, these tended to be small in relation to differences between people with different qualifications.

There was a strong correlation between the number of O grades young people had at the end of the fourth year at school and the likelihood of their being in a full-time job in the spring after leaving school (Table 3.2). In each year, those with the most SCE passes were most likely to be working full-time. In the spring of 1981, for example, 57 per cent of males and 49 per cent of females with no O grade passes were in full-time jobs: this compared with 87 per cent of males and 67 per cent of females with five or more O grades. By 1987, far fewer young people were in full-time jobs in the spring following school leaving. However, those with five or more O grades were still the most likely to be in full-time jobs while those with no O grade passes were least likely to have been working full-time.

Throughout the 1980s, those who left school without O grade passes were more likely than qualified leavers to be unemployed in the spring after leaving school. In 1981 around one in five (21 per cent of males and 23 per cent of females) of the unqualified leavers were unemployed; and this had increased to nearly three in ten (27 per cent of males and females) by 1987. In comparison,

TABLE 3.2 Spring destinations of minimum-age school-leavers, by fourth year SCE passes: 1981-1987 (%)

	Schemes Male Female		Job Male Female		Unemployed Male Female		Education Male Female		Other Male Female		Unweighted n Male Female		Total Male Female	
DE/No Award														
1981	20	18	57	49	21	23	2	8	*	1	(475)	(519)	100	99
1983	27	28	39	32	28	26	2	9	3	5	(1272)	(1041)	99	100
1985	32	27	32	32	30	28	2	6	3	7	(896)	(699)	99	100
1987	45	40	23	20	27	27	2	7	3	6	(539)	(461)	100	100
1-2 0 Grades														
1981	17	16	68	55	12	11	3	17	0	1	(454)	(417)	100	100
1983	24	23	57	35	12	12	5	24	2	6	(425)	(349)	100	100
1985	38	28	41	40	16	15	3	14	2	3	(401)	(369)	100	100
1987	51	43	28	26	16	13	3	14	2	4	(264)	(267)	100	100
3-4 0 Grades														
1981	10	8	80	61	6	6	4	24	0	1	(235)	(232)	100	100
1983	12	15	70	49	8	9	9	22	1	6	(173)	(185)	100	101
1985	38	22	44	41	12	12	6	21	1	4	(222)	(225)	101	101
1987	49	41	37	25	10	7	4	22	0	4	(163)	(185)	100	99
5+ 0 Grades														
1981	4	13	87	67	4	1	4	18	1	1	(135)	(118)	100	99
1983	9	13	79	53	6	9	3	23	3	2	(83)	(58)	100	100
1985	22	25	59	47	10	8	7	14	2	6	(164)	(134)	100	100
1987	35	35	48	37	7	4	7	20	3	3	(102)	(129)	100	99

Note: * less than 0.5 per cent.

very few well qualified leavers were unemployed. In 1981, for example, just 4 per cent of males and 1 per cent of females with five or more O grades were unemployed. By 1987 unemployment within this group had increased by three percentage points for males and females (to 7 per cent of males and 4 per cent of females).

The pattern of participation on schemes was also skewed towards the less qualified: in 1981 around one in five unqualified leavers were on schemes in the spring after leaving school (20 per cent of males and 18 per cent of females) as compared with 4 per cent of males and 13 per cent of females with five or more O grades. Scheme participation expanded throughout the decade, but this expansion occurred mainly among the lower qualified. By 1987, 45 per cent of males and 40 per cent of females with no O grade passes were on YTS, yet among those with five or more O grades, just over a third were on YTS (35 per cent of males and females).

In Chapter 2 I argued that despite various 'reforms' of the education system, differences in young people's educational attainments continued to be strongly affected by their social class of origin. While class differences in educational attainment may have been reduced over the last decade or so, it is important to examine whether class differences in post-school destinations have changed over the last decade, as qualifications are only of value in so far as they can be 'traded' in the labour market.

Over the decade 1977 to 1987 there were quite strong class-based differences in young people's post-school destinations (Hoskins *et al.*, 1989; Furlong, 1990a). Between 1977 and 1987, minimum-age school-leavers from lower working-class families in Scotland were always less likely to be in a full-time job in the spring after leaving than were those from other social classes. Over the decade, young people from the lower working-class were also more likely than those from other classes to be unemployed in the spring after leaving and were more likely to be on work experience and training schemes (although here the differences between the lower working-class and the upper working-class were not as great).

The existence of class-based differences in school- leavers' destinations is not surprising given the links between social class and educational attainment because qualifications give young people advantages in the labour market (Ashton *et al.*, 1982; Gray *et al.*,

TABLE 3.3 Spring destinations of minimum-age school-leavers, by social class: 1977–1987 (%)

	Schemes Male	Schemes Female	Job Male	Job Female	Unemployed Male	Unemployed Female	Education Male	Education Female	Other Male	Other Female	Unweighted n Male	Unweighted n Female	Total Male	Total Female
Professional & Managerial Class														
1977+	1	2	86	64	9	10	2	19	1	4	(127)	(110)	99	99
1979	7	4	81	68	6	6	6	20	*	2	(204)	(216)	100	100
1981	9	4	80	63	7	11	3	21	1	1	(194)	(145)	100	100
1983	19	14	62	36	11	16	6	28	3	5	(211)	(175)	101	99
1985	26	24	56	44	10	15	7	13	1	4	(202)	(145)	100	100
1987	44	32	35	27	14	19	4	20	3	2	(151)	(143)	100	100
% change 1977–1987	+43	+30	-51	-37	+5	+9	+2	+1	+2	-2				
Upper Working Class														
1977+	7	3	75	74	14	13	2	7	2	3	(610)	(570)	100	100
1979	8	8	80	72	10	9	1	9	1	2	(860)	(854)	100	100
1981	20	17	62	53	16	17	2	11	*	1	(771)	(726)	100	99
1983	24	26	50	37	20	18	3	14	2	5	(1031)	(801)	99	100
1985	36	27	38	40	20	19	2	11	3	4	(679)	(587)	99	101
1987	48	43	31	25	17	14	3	12	2	5	(456)	(460)	101	99
% change 1977–1987	+41	+40	-44	-49	+3	+1	+1	+5	0	+2				
Lower Working Class														
1977+	7	3	71	69	20	18	1	6	2	3	(245)	(275)	101	99
1979	7	6	71	68	14	15	2	9	*	2	(416)	(439)	99	100
1981	19	21	54	49	23	17	2	11	1	1	(350)	(378)	99	99
1983	28	25	47	38	20	19	1	11	4	7	(397)	(367)	100	100
1985	30	26	41	38	25	18	2	11	3	7	(325)	(272)	101	100
1987	52	41	21	27	22	17	2	8	2	7	(178)	(191)	99	100
% change 1977–1987	+45	+38	-50	-42	+2	-1	+1	+2	0	+4				

Notes: 1. + 1977 figures are based on four regions (Strathclyde, Lothian, Fife and Tayside).

1983; Furlong and Raffe, 1989; Lee *et al.*, 1990). However, it is important to examine whether these differences in the experiences of young people from different social classes have changed over the decade. In terms of jobs and schemes, patterns of inequality in Scotland have changed little. The percentage fall in the proportion of young people who were in full-time jobs in the spring between 1977 and 1987 was similar for all classes (Furlong, 1990a) (Table 3.3). The proportion of young people from the professional and managerial class who were in full-time jobs fell by 46 percentage points, while for young people from the upper working-class and lower working-class it fell by 47 percentage points and 46 percentage points respectively.

If we look at participation in work experience and training schemes in terms of social class, it is clear that the level of participation among young people from the professional and managerial class was always lower than among young people from other classes and this differential has been maintained. This finding has also emerged from other studies of training schemes. Raffe (1984b) and Seale (1985), for example, have both shown that the social composition of schemes has tended to be biased towards young people with fathers employed in manual occupations. Furthermore, over the decade young people from the professional and managerial class tended to trail behind those from other classes in their uptake of scheme places. There were large increases in scheme participation among young people from the working-classes between 1979 and 1981, and again between 1983 and 1985, and between 1985 and 1987. For those from the professional and managerial class the first main increase came later, between 1981 and 1983, and then increased relatively slowly until between 1985 and 1987 when participation increased at a similar rate to those from the other classes (Furlong, 1990a). In 1977, school-leavers from the professional and managerial class were less likely to be unemployed than those from either of the other classes, yet the differentials between the classes in respect to unemployment narrowed over the decade and young people from professional and managerial families (especially females) became increasingly vulnerable to unemployment.

In this section I have described some of the changes in the post-school destinations of minimum-age school-leavers in Scotland over the decade 1977 to 1987. The youth labour market changed over this decade in that there was a sharp fall in the proportion of school-leavers who entered full-time jobs after school and a rise in the proportion who were unemployed or on schemes. Although young people's routes into the labour market tended to have become more complex, there were important sources of continuity in the youth labour market. In particular, it was evident that young people from privileged social backgrounds and those with qualifications continued to be advantaged within the labour market. In the next section, I look in more detail at the sorts of jobs young people entered and examine the relative influence of social class and qualifications on their chances of entering different types of occupation.

3.3 Social class, qualifications and 'respectable' jobs

By 1983 less than half of the young people who left school at the minimum age were reporting themselves as being in full-time jobs by the spring after leaving. Schemes were rapidly becoming an established route into the labour market, but because schemes had become a normal part of the typical post-school experience, it makes it difficult to comment on trends in occupational entry using data collected ten months after the majority had left school. At present, the only occupational measure we have for many young people is that of YTS placement occupation. This is unsatisfactory as young people may change occupations on leaving their schemes. However, longitudinal work on young people in Scotland has shown that there is a high level of continuity between YTS placements and subsequent occupations (Furlong and Raffe, 1989).[4] This gives some credibility to the approach I adopt here, which uses the occupation reported in the spring after leaving school, irrespective of whether this was a 'real' job or a scheme.

While we need to be a little cautious of combining 'real' jobs with schemes, I would suggest that a young person's first occupation is still a good indicator of their future life chances. Young people's chances of being kept on by their YTS sponsor or employer varied between occupations and industries, but post-scheme occupational mobility tended to be short-wave and rarely crossed broad occupational divisions. For example, young people who were trainees in sales occupations (who had a relatively low chance of being kept on by their employer at the end of the scheme) often found employment as operatives and labourers (Furlong and Raffe, 1989). Here I use a simple dichotomy to describe young people's occupations because it is necessary to look at the broad occupational groups within which young people share common life-chances.

The literature on young people's occupational orientations has tended to highlight a basic distinction between 'respectable' jobs ('respectable' in middle-class terms), which offer a degree of security and job satisfaction, and 'shit jobs' which offer little in the way of career development or inherent job satisfaction (Jenkins, 1983; Coffield *et al.*, 1986; Brown, 1987b). Young people who wish to enter 'respectable' jobs may be willing to put some effort into their school work in order to fulfil any entrance requirements, yet not all young people will necessarily aspire to these jobs or feel that it is worthwhile to put themselves out in order to obtain such jobs. Willis (1977), for example, regards the orientation towards low-skill jobs as being part of a rejection of 'authority' and of the middle-class values embodied in the school. Ashton and Field (1976) suggest that young people from lower working-class homes are not culturally predisposed to postpone immediate gratification in order to enter a situation where rewards are deferred. Yet attitudes towards work are not always clear-cut or strongly conditioned by prior orientations. Young people may enter less skilled jobs for more pragmatic reasons such as the financial inducement of high starting wages, as compared with young people employed as apprentices who take some years to reach their full earnings potential (Jenkins, 1983).

In this chapter I have classified jobs as either 'respectable' jobs or as 'low-skill' jobs. The 'low-skill' category includes semi- and unskilled manual work and routine shop work.[5] This sort of work rarely provides opportunities for advancement and has been described as 'careerless' work (Ashton and Field, 1976). In contrast to 'low-skill' jobs, 'respectable' jobs usually provide some opportunity for career advancement as well as higher status and a greater level of job security. The 'respectable' jobs category includes managerial, professional and related occupations, and technical, clerical and skilled manual jobs. These sorts of jobs have been termed respectively 'long-term career jobs' and 'working-class career jobs' (Ashton and Field, 1976), (although relatively few minimum-age school-leavers entered 'long-term career jobs').

Over the decade 1977 to 1987, the proportion of minimum-age school-leavers who entered 'respectable' jobs either as employees or as trainees declined. Females tended to be affected by this decline to a greater extent than males; the proportion of females

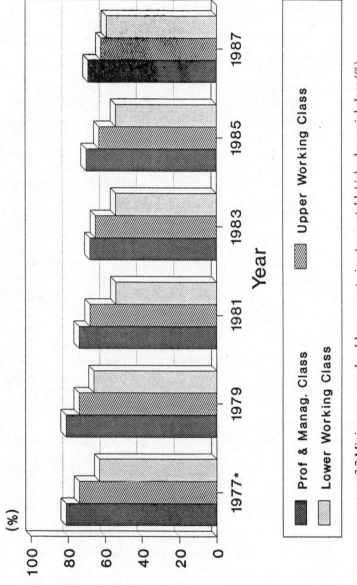

FIGURE 3.2 Minimum-age school-leavers entering 'respectable' jobs, by social class (%). 1977 figures are based on four regions, Strathclyde, Lothian, Fife and Tayside.

entering 'respectable' jobs declined by 18 percentage points (from 65 per cent to 47 per cent), while for males the proportion declined by 7 percentage points (from 67 per cent to 60 per cent). The greatest part of this decline occurred between 1979 and 1985. Across the decade strong differentials persisted in the types of jobs entered by young people from different social classes. There was always a greater proportion of young people from the professional and managerial class who entered 'respectable' jobs, followed by those from the upper working-class, with those from the lower working-class consistently obtaining the lowest proportion (Figure 3.2). The difference between the lower working-class and the professional and managerial class fluctuated between years, but the net change, either across the decade or between 1979 and 1987, did not result in wider class differentials. Between 1977 and 1987, the difference between the lower working-class and the professional and managerial class narrowed by 8 points (from a difference of 18 percentage points to 10 percentage points), while if we take the years 1979 to 1987 the differential narrowed by 5 percentage points (from 15 percentage points to 10 percentage points) (Furlong, 1990a).

Because the influence of class on young people's prospects of entering a particular occupational levels tends to be mediated through educational attainments (Heath, 1981), changes in the occupational distributions of school-leavers from different classes may be a result of the changes in relative educational successes which were discussed in the previous chapter. Among the different school-leaver groups there was a relationship between qualifications and entry into 'respectable' jobs. In each year, young people with qualifications were most likely to have entered 'respectable' jobs, although in 1981, for males, it was having any O grade passes rather than the number of O grade passes which was important for entry. Between 1981 and 1987 the fall in the overall proportion entering 'respectable' jobs had the greatest effect on the lower qualified group. While there was little change among young men with over three O grades in the proportion entering 'respectable' jobs, the proportion entering with one or two O grades fell by 16 percentage points, while the proportion entering with no awards (of whom relatively few entered such jobs even in 1981) fell by 4 percentage points. For females, the fall was less severe among those with no O grades and with one or two O grades, but whereas there was an increase in the proportion of

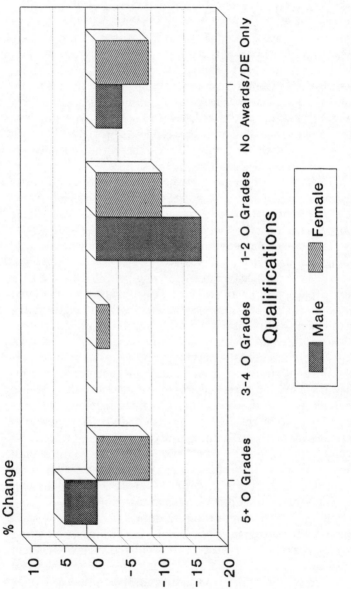

FIGURE 3.3 Change in the proportion of young people entering 'respectable' jobs between 1981 and 1987, by total qualifications

males who entered 'respectable' jobs, for females there was a decline of 8 percentage points (Figure 3.3).

Among the males, much of the decline in the proportion who entered 'respectable' jobs was attributable to the decline in apprenticeships. In 1977, just over half of all male minimum-age school-leavers (51 per cent) who were in jobs or on schemes in the spring after leaving school reported that they were apprentices. Apprenticeship entry declined sharply between 1981 and 1987, and had the greatest effect on school-leavers with one or two O grades. In comparison to the qualified leavers, those with no O grades were less likely to have been apprenticed, but the rate of decline between 1981 and 1987 (18 percentage points) was similar to the rate of decline among those with three or four O grades and five or more O grades (15 and 16 percentage points respectively). In 1981, those with one or two O grades were almost as likely as those with more O grades to have entered an apprenticeship, yet the apprenticeship entry among this group declined at such a rate (by 27 percentage points) that by 1987 the difference in apprenticeship entry between those with one or two O grades and those with three or four O grades was 17 percentage points (36 per cent and 53 per cent respectively).

I have described the ways in which changes in the youth labour market have affected young people from different social backgrounds and with different levels of school achievement, but in order to look at the relative influences of each of the factors I have described on young people's chances of entering 'respectable' jobs it is necessary to use multivariate analysis. In a recent paper (Furlong, 1990a) I constructed a logit model (Wrigley, 1985) to predict the relative chances of certain 'types' of minimum-age school-leaver having entered a 'respectable' job by the spring after school leaving.[6] The first conclusion was that the relative chances of females from the upper working-class having entered a 'respectable' job in 1977 was significantly lower than for females from the professional and managerial class. For males the picture was rather different. Those from the upper working-class were more likely than those from the professional and managerial class to have entered a 'respectable' job, while those from the lower working-class were marginally less likely to have done so. To test whether the influence of class on the chances of getting a 'respectable' job had changed during the course of the decade, I added a class by year interaction to the model; it did not have a significant effect.

The second finding was that for both males and females qualifications were shown to have had a powerful effect on the chances
of entering a 'respectable' job, and relative chances were found to
decline in line with qualifications. While the difference between
males or females with five or more O grades and three or four O
grades was relatively small, those with either one or two O grades
or with no passes at grades A-C were at a significant disadvantage. Indeed, the chances of males with one or two O grades
having entered a 'respectable' job were half that of males with five
or more O grades, while females with one or two O grades had
their relative chances reduced by around 60 per cent. Those with
no O grade passes had very little chance of entering a 'respectable' job, but the chances for males and females were similar.

The effects of social class and educational attainment are com-
pounded by the effects of the decline in the youth labour market
in different years. Thus, in 1979 the relative chances of entering a
'respectable' job declined by a factor of one (for both males and
females), and continued to decline for much of the decade. Although
the relative chances of males and females were similar in 1979, the
decline in the youth labour market had a much more dramatic
effect on females who saw their chances of obtaining 'respectable'
jobs halved by 1981. Opportunities for males did not fall as much
and fell at a much slower pace (Furlong, 1990a).

3.4 The unemployed

This chapter is concerned with aspects of change and continuity
in the youth transition over the past decade, and any discussion of
differential labour market outcomes over the decade up to 1987
must include an assessment of changes in the likelihood of unemployment among different groups. This poses another dilemma as
there are a number of problems in comparing unemployment
rates of 17-year-olds because of the extent of the changes in the
youth labour market over this period. Youth training schemes
have become a central part of the transitional experiences of minimum-age school-leavers. In 1977 they were typically six-month
schemes, but they subsequently changed to a year's duration and
later to two years'.

It is misleading to try and make comparisons as the chances of
young people being unemployed are affected by the availability
and duration of schemes. In 1977, for example, someone who
joined a six-month scheme in the autumn could have been unem-

ployed again by the spring. In 1987 it had become less likely that someone would be unemployed six months after joining the new, two-year, Youth Training Scheme. Not only was the scheme duration longer, but those who left without a job to go to risked losing their social security benefit. In order to maintain some level of comparability I have confined my analysis of unemployment to an examination of minimum-age school-leavers who were unemployed in the spring after school-leaving, who had not been on a work experience or training scheme and who had not had a job since leaving school. These are described as the 'long-term unemployed' as they had a much greater experience of unemployment than their peers.

A relatively small proportion of school-leavers were defined as 'long-term unemployed' in comparison to those who were unemployed at any one time. Although the Government has attempted to abolish long-term school-leaver unemployment, among the Scottish cohort the long-term unemployed doubled from 3 per cent in 1979 to 6 per cent in 1987 (Furlong, 1990a). Moreover, much of the increase in long-term unemployment was among unqualified school-leavers. Among those with no O grades, for example, long-term unemployment rose by 6 percentage points, while among those with five or more O grades it rose by just 1 percentage point. There was no clear pattern of variation along the lines of social class.

Again it is necessary to use a multivariate model to disentangle the effects of social class and qualifications on long-term unemployment and I have used a logit model to examine the relative chances of long-term unemployment among minimum-age school-leavers in the spring after school leaving.[7] The effects of social class on the relative chances of long-term unemployment were found to be small and not statistically significant. The addition of a class by year interaction, in order to assess whether the effects of class on a young person's chances of long-term unemployment had changed over time, also proved not to be significant (Furlong, 1990a). This suggests that the effects of social class on the probability of long-term unemployment has not changed significantly since 1979.

This analysis demonstrates the vulnerability of those with few school-leaving qualifications to long-term unemployment. Males with no O grade passes, for example, had relative chances of long-term unemployment which were nearly three times greater than

those with five or more O grades. Females with no O grade passes
were twice as likely as those with five or more O grades to experience long-term unemployment. The relative chances of long- term
unemployment also increased with time and became more serious
for females. In 1987, for example, young women's chances of
long-term unemployment were around two-and-a-half times
greater than in 1979, while young men's chances had increased by
about 80 per cent (Furlong, 1990a).

During the 1980s, unemployment had a considerable effect on
young people making the transition from school to work. Even
those without personal experience of unemployment made plans
within, and were constrained by, the declining opportunities in
the labour market. In this discussion of unemployment I have
confined the analysis to those who had been continuously unemployed by the spring after school leaving. To a large extent I have
been looking at the tip of the iceberg; I will return to discuss
unemployment in greater detail in Chapter 5.

3.5 Conclusion

In this chapter I have highlighted some important aspects of
change and continuity in the youth transition over the decade
1977 to 1987. I have suggested that the 'old' transition in which a
majority of school-leavers were in full-time employment soon
after leaving school has disappeared and a new, 'protracted',
transition has emerged in which few young people are in employment in the period immediately after leaving school. The new
transition is characterised by mass unemployment, under-
employment and increased participation in education and training schemes by young people trying to escape the dole. Despite
these trends, the increased protraction of the transition and the
proliferation of training schemes and courses seems to have
brought few benefits.

For the young people who were making their transition from
school during this period, there were two trends which had far-
reaching implications. The first of these concerned the adverse
effects of the changes in the youth labour market on young
women: their chances of entering 'respectable' jobs declined seriously over the decade, and their chances of long-term unemployment in the immediate post-school period increased to a greater
extent than for males. The second trend affected both males and
females. This was the qualification inflation which had its most

visible impact on those with one or two O grades. In 1977 these young people enjoyed a relatively advantaged position in the labour market: their qualifications helped them avoid long- term unemployment and they had a relatively good chance of securing 'respectable' jobs. By 1987, the position of those with one or two O grades had declined and their advantage over those with no O grade passes had been reduced.

Despite these changes, there were some important similarities between 1977 and 1987. Throughout the decade it was young people with poor qualifications who suffered the worst effects of the collapse of the youth labour market. Those from the lower social classes often had an added disadvantage, although when I controlled for qualifications I found that, in relative terms, the young people from working-class homes were neither more vulnerable nor more advantaged in 1987 than they were in 1977. Despite the advances made by young people from the working-classes in terms of qualifications, the links between education and social class remained strong. Those with poor qualifications were frequently young people from the working-class.

Notes

1. It is also likely that women's participation in post-compulsory education has been accelerated by the increasing importance of credentials in the female labour market.
2. Although minimum-aged school-leavers are declining as a proportion of all school-leavers, this group has traditionally made a fairly direct transition from school to work It is important to look in detail at the ways in which changes in the youth labour market have affected young people following a pattern which has been considered 'normal' among working-class and lower qualified groups who are known to have been particularly vulnerable to unemployment over this period.
3. As these figures are based on 'snapshots' taken in the spring after the majority had left school, the figures are affected by the increase in the length of schemes from six months to a year. Some participants on the six-month scheme will have re-entered the labour market by the spring after school-leaving.
4. Continuity was noted in relation to YTS placements and subsequent employment. The relationship between YOP placements and subsequent employment may have been different.
5. Warwick Occupational Categories 1 through 10 and 12 through 17 have been classed as 'respectable' jobs, and categories 11, 18, 19 and 23 as 'low-skill' jobs.
6. Full details are provided in Appendix II.
7. Full details are provided in Appendix II.

4
YOUTH TRAINING SCHEMES AND THE TRANSITION

4.1 Introduction

In the discussion of recent changes in the youth transition it became apparent that one of the most important changes in the transition from school to work was brought about as a result of the introduction of work experience and training schemes, which by 1987 had become the principal destination of minimum-aged school-leavers. A majority of minimum-aged school-leavers now experience youth training schemes in Britain. Because the Youth Training Scheme (YTS) was intended as a scheme which would equip young people with vocational skills and training, any discussion of the transition from school to work must explore the role of schemes in the transition in order both to examine what it is that trainees are learning, and to identify the likely outcomes of the YTS experience. In particular, it is important to find out if YTS is affecting young people's subsequent career paths, or whether their post-YTS labour market experiences could have been predicted on the basis of school achievement.

In order to understand the effects of YTS on the transition from school to work, it is important to understand something of its history as YTS is essentially a product of the rise in youth unemployment which occurred in the 1970s and which gave birth to the schemes which preceded it. The increase in youth unemployment in Britain throughout the 1970s prompted Government intervention in the form of job creation schemes for the unemployed. In part the schemes developed out of fears of increasing levels of hooliganism and delinquency (Sinfield, 1981), as well as from motives of concern that young people were becoming frustrated and disillusioned and that work was a habit caught early or not at all. In 1975 the Manpower Services Commission set up the Job Creation Programme with the aim of providing short-term jobs of social value for unemployed young people. The scheme was intended not to create permanent jobs, but to maintain the employability of the individual until they were able to find employment (Holland, 1977). The Job Creation Programme was abandoned in 1978, but during the three years in which it operated, 200,000 young people participated in the programme.

In April 1978 the Youth Opportunities Programme was launched to supersede the Job Creation Programme. This was largely a result of the Holland Report (1977) which contained an appreciation of the structural factors underlying youth unemployment: 'Success or failure in getting a job is often a matter of luck and is frequently determined by factors well beyond the control or achievement of the individual such as the state of the national economy, the local industrial structure or the kind of preparation for work available at school' (Holland, 1977, p. 33). While the Job Creation Programme had been concerned to maintain employability until a cyclical upturn in the economy, the Youth Opportunities Programme (YOP) was designed to 'enable the individual to do more things, achieve a higher level of skills, knowledge and performance, and adapt more readily to changing circumstances or job requirements' (Holland, 1977, p. 34). Although the philosophical principles which underpinned YOP resulted in an emphasis being placed on tackling the causes of youth unemployment rather than the consequences, Raffe (1983c) has suggested that the approach still tended to explain youth unemployment in terms of individual characteristics; Holland regarded increasing skill levels as a solution to unemployment, and poor preparation at school was seen as a factor which increased individual vulnerability.

The Youth Opportunities Programme was an unemployment-based scheme; to become eligible for a place, young people had to have been unemployed for a minimum of six weeks. In the main, YOP was delivered through six-month work experience placements with an employer for which the young person was paid a tax-free allowance set slightly above the unemployment rate. The Programme was widely criticised for providing little in the way of training for young people, while providing employers with a free source of labour (Cohen, 1982; Stafford, 1981; Watts, 1983). At this time the whole context of industrial training was at the forefront of debate owing to the economic recession and owing to fears that Britain was lagging behind its industrial competitors partly because of inadequate training for the young. In response to this debate, the Manpower Services Commission developed its New

Training Initiative which aimed to improve the training of the British workforce (MSC, 1981).

The Youth Training Scheme was the part of the New Training Initiative which was concerned to improve the training of young people by giving them the opportunity to enter post-16 education, training, or a period of planned work experience which would include elements of off-the-job training. The Manpower Services Commission (MSC) had envisaged the Youth Training Scheme as a 'permanent bridge between school and work'. The scheme was intended as a twelve-month broad-based, high-quality course of vocational preparation and training. It was to include a minimum of three months' off-the-job training for all trainees. Training was not to be job-specific, but was to go beyond the needs of the job through the learning of core skills which were transferable within a 'family' of occupations and which could be built on in later years.

In practice, a compromise was reached when it came to implementing the new scheme which resulted in YTS having both a training and an unemployment function. While MSC had envisaged YTS as a training initiative available to all young people whether employed or unemployed, the Government was primarily concerned with providing training for unemployed school-leavers. Consequently, the emphasis of the scheme changed from what was intended as a comprehensive training scheme, to a measure for dealing with the unemployed (Hockley, 1984). In 1986 the scheme was extended to two years (although most of the discussion in this chapter is focused on the 1985 cohort of the Scottish Young People's Survey, most of whom entered the one-year YTS) and in 1991 Youth Training (YT) (a slightly more flexible scheme with greater emphasis placed on 'employee status' trainees) superseded YTS.

4.2 Schemes as transitional routes

Over the last decade, schemes have become important routes between school and work for an increasingly large proportion of school-leavers. Although schemes provide a route which most early school-leavers will follow at some point, few of the better qualified school-leavers will experience YTS. Furthermore, schemes tend to be stratified so that unqualified school-leavers and those with good leaving qualifications are unlikely to enter the same sorts of scheme. The stratification of youth training has implications for young people's post-scheme experiences as well as for our theoretical understanding of the role of schemes in the transition.

Both YOP and YTS recruited heavily from among young people with few educational qualifications. In a survey of over 3,000 young people who had joined YOP (Bedeman and Harvey, 1981), 71 per cent were found to have no O level passes. Under YTS, just over half (53 per cent) of the members of the 1985 Scottish cohort who experienced YTS had no O grade passes (Furlong and Raffe, 1989), although a higher proportion of trainees on YTS had O grade passes than was the case under YOP (Raffe, 1988b). This increase in the qualifications held by trainees is to be expected, because under the regulations young people had to be unemployed to join YOP, while YTS was open to all minimum-age school-leavers and a large proportion of older leavers. Raffe (1988b) has argued that the capability of .YTS to recruit from among young people with 'middle-range' qualifications means that it has been successful in 'attracting' some qualified school-leavers who will have joined YTS in preference to 'ordinary jobs'.

It is true that some of the young people who entered YTS would have been in a relatively strong position in the labour market had they decided to apply for low-skill jobs. However, it is wrong to use this evidence to suggest that YTS is 'attracting' higher qualified school-leavers. Occupational socialisation in the home and the school results in school-leavers having their sights set on a particular 'band' of occupations. A young person who had expectations of entering an apprenticeship, for example, would be unlikely to make any deliberate 'choice' between, say, an unskilled job and a training scheme offering the chance of apprentice training. Such a young person would be likely to seek a 'proper' apprenticeship in the first place and to take a YTS scheme which offered the chance of being allowed to complete an apprenticeship if the first objective was unsuccessful (Furlong, 1987). The increasing qualifications of YTS trainees does not reflect the ability of YTS to 'attract' qualified school leavers. Rather, the trend reflects the increasing domination of the youth labour market by YTS and the establishment of a distinctive YTS 'foothold' in the middle range of the youth job market.

As YTS became prominent in the middle sector of the youth labour market, schemes tended to become increasingly stratified. Within YOP there was a division between the low-status training

workshops and community schemes, and the more common
Work Experience on Employers' Premises (WEEP) which offered
greater advantages in terms of subsequent employment opportunities. Within WEEP there were placements which were recognised as of poor quality with little chance of trainees being
kept on, as well as placements which provided better-quality
training and good prospects of subsequent employment. The picture
under YTS (and YT) is similar in that there is a fairly clear hierarchy of schemes, although there is an additional rung at the top
of the hierarchy composed of 'employee-status' trainees who are
part of a firm's core workforce even while on YTS. Furthermore,
Lee and colleagues (1990) have shown that 'top' schemes are often
openly selective, placing a high value on academic and social
criteria, while other schemes tend to 'mop up' the unqualified and
disadvantaged.

Roberts and Parsell (1989) have identified three distinct sectors
of Youth Training Scheme: the sponsored sector; the contest sector;
and 'sink schemes'. At the top of the hierarchy, the trainees in the
sponsored sector either have 'employee status' from the start, or
know that they have a very strong chance of a permanent job at
the end of the scheme. This type of scheme often provides routes
into sought-after careers such as apprenticeships. Many of the
better qualified YTS entrants join sponsored schemes. This sector
has increased in importance as levels of youth unemployment
have begun to fall, and is a particularly important sector in parts
of the country with low unemployment. According to figures
issued by the Training Agency,[1] the number of trainees with
employee status rose from 11 per cent in March 1987 to just over
22 per cent in March 1989 (Training Agency, 1989a). However,
fewer trainees have employee status in Scotland, Wales and
Northern Ireland than in the Midlands and the South of England
(Training Agency, 1989b).

Those who enter the 'contest' sector face less certainty. Trainees expect to gain skills, experience and qualifications which they
hope will enhance their employment prospects at the end of the
scheme. They may be successful in winning a permanent position
in the firm where they have been trained; alternatively, their skills
and experience may strengthen their position in the external labour
market. Many of the firms who use the Youth Training Scheme
use it as a method of screening potential recruits (Ashton *et al.*,
1982; Lee *et al.*, 1990). Employers may take 'suitable' trainees into

their permanent workforce when vacancies arise, or may make routine decisions on retention when trainees come to the end of their time on the scheme.

At the bottom of the hierarchy of YTS schemes are those labelled as 'sink schemes' by Roberts and Parsell (1989). In the main these are community schemes where the chances of being kept on are virtually non-existent. Raffe (1987) describes these schemes as the 'detached sector' as they are detached from the process of selection and recruitment within the labour market.

In general, school-leavers with the highest qualifications who join YTS enter those schemes which have the best record of trainee recruitment and placement. The poorest qualified trainees are more likely to enter schemes based in the community, rather than employer-led schemes (Roberts and Parsell, 1989). Indeed, the sorts of young people who are placed on community schemes tend to be those who would be difficult to place with employers (Roberts and Parsell, 1989). They also include a disproportionate number of black trainees, and tend to be more common in areas of high unemployment.

One of the most visible aspects of the stratification of youth training is the differences in the sorts of occupation in which males and females are trained. These differences reinforce gender stereotyping of occupations and help ensure that women remain in low-paid, low-status occupations (Cockburn, 1987). Figure 4.1 is extracted from the Training Agency's 'Youth Training News' (Training Agency, 1989a) and clearly shows the gender segregation of training. In February 1989, 60 per cent of young males were being trained in three occupational groups, (construction, engineering and motor vehicle repair). Less than 3 per cent of females were being trained in these occupations. In contrast, 60 per cent of females were being trained in two different occupations (office work and community health), while only 10 per cent of males were being trained in these occupations.

These figures present a picture of sex segregation which is even more severe than the one presented by Cockburn from the MSC's statistics. Yet Cockburn has shown that in ten of the eleven 'Occupational Training Families' used by the MSC, the sex ratio of young workers was more extreme than 70:30.

The sex segregation of schemes reflects both the sexual segregation of the wider labour market and the preferences of young people on leaving school – preferences which are shaped within

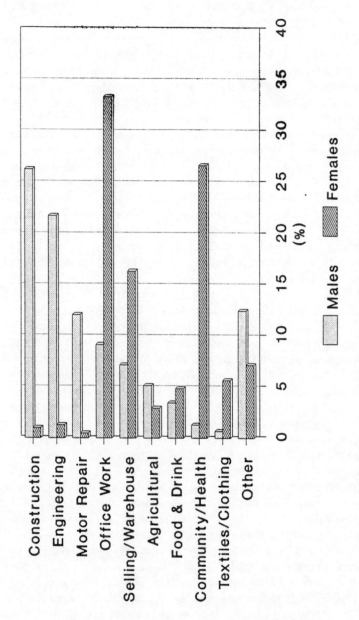

FIGURE 4.1 Trainees occupational classification, February 1989. Source: Training Agency.

the constraints of a segmented labour market. Those responsible for the delivery of the scheme may dislike the pattern of segmentation in YTS, but typically feel that at the age of sixteen it is 'too late': 'Young women come to us *asking* for office jobs, nursery work, hairdressing. What can we do about it ? We can't force them to do something they don't want to do' (Cockburn, 1987, p. 197). While sex discrimination undoubtedly exists in scheme recruitment, Cockburn argues that it tends to be passive discrimination which, owing to the delegation of responsibility for delivery of YTS to a number of employers and managing agents, tends to be outside of the control of the MSC. Nevertheless, the scheme may be regarded as a wasted opportunity: as a forum through which the walls separating the male and female segments of the labour market could gradually be dismantled, given the commitment.

In research which focused on female trainees, Bates (1989) identified a pattern of downward adjustment of occupational aspirations among trainees. She suggested that young women's ambitions get 'cooled-out' several times during the course of the new, 'prolonged' transition, and that they eventually apply for the less desirable jobs and schemes. In her study of a group of 16-18-year-old females training for the 'caring' occupations, she found that at first the young women aimed for the more desirable 'caring' occupations such as nursery nursing, but eventually they became socialised to jobs lower down the hierarchy such as care assistants. However, Bates offers no evidence to show that the 'prolonged' transition results in a greater 'cooling-out' than under the old more direct transition, or that this has any implications for the distribution of women in the occupational hierarchy.

There is a considerable variation among occupations in the extent to which employers have been willing to participate in YTS. In recent years YTS has become an established route into skilled trades, and in some industries (such as construction), trade agreements have meant that all apprentices spend the first part of their apprenticeships as YTS trainees (although some will have employee status while others run the risk of not being kept on).

Among the Scottish cohort, a higher proportion of minimum-aged school-leavers on YTS were working in craft and skilled manual occupations (29 per cent) in the spring after leaving school than were those in 'ordinary' jobs (20 per cent) (Furlong and Raffe, 1989). Trainees were also used extensively in shops, and a higher proportion of YTS trainees worked in sales jobs (19 per cent) than 'ordinary' employees (8 per cent). In contrast, young people working as operatives and labourers were more likely to be 'ordin-ary' employees (38 per cent) than trainees (21 per cent).

Although one can identify types of schemes on the basis of the ways in which they relate to the labour market, schemes train young people for different sorts of jobs and do so with varying degrees of efficiency. The effectiveness of schemes is related both to the type of training given and the quality of that training as well as to the sorts of jobs young people are being trained for. In 1985, 80 per cent of the Scottish cohort said that they were given some training whilst on their schemes. Just over one in ten (11 per cent) said that they were receiving apprentice training.[2] 60 per cent of those who experienced YTS said that they gained a YTS leaving certificate.[3] In addition 30 per cent gained at least one Scotvec module, and 11 per cent gained other qualifications such as City and Guilds certificates.

Much of the training carried out through YTS is strongly voca-tional. Training Agency (1989c) figures show that around 95 per cent of qualifications gained on YTS were classed as 'vocational'. Vocational qualifications tend to be occupationally specific and their value is determined by employers as occupational 'gate-keepers'. In order to gain qualifications while on YTS it is often necessary for young people to complete their schemes.[4] Informa-tion from the YTS Leavers' Surveys (Training Agency, 1988a) shows that over 60 per cent of trainees who remained on YTS for two years gained qualifications, in comparison to 30 per cent of those who left before the end of the first year.

Young people were generally rather sceptical about the trans-ferability of skills learnt through courses taken on YTS. Among the Scottish cohort, few young people (13 per cent) agreed 'very much' that the courses they took while on YTS made it easier for them to transfer from one job to another. In the main, young people tended to feel that the most important benefit of their YTS courses was in preparing them for future work and in making them better at doing a particular job. However, there was some evidence that YTS courses articulated with other training they received; young people often expressed the view that YTS courses fitted well with other training and experience (Furlong and Raffe, 1989). To be of value, training does not have to be certified, nor does it have to result in occupationally specific skills. Many train-ees believed that their personal effectiveness had been improved as a result of their YTS experience. Research conducted by the Training Agency (1988b) shows that over 70 per cent of trainees said that YTS helped them 'get on better with people'; nearly 80 per cent said that YTS had helped them 'become more confident'; and over 80 per cent said that YTS had 'helped them to understand more about jobs'.

4.3 YTS and the labour market

The stratification of schemes and their position in the broader labour market has implications for recruitment and young people's positions in the adult labour market. In Chapter 8 I will look more closely at the implications of YTS experience on the occupations young people subsequently entered. In this chapter, I will consider two performance indicators of YTS which have implications for young people's careers. These relate first to the immediate post-YTS destinations of ex-trainees, and second, to the chances of ex-trainees being in employment a couple of years after having left YTS. Judged by young people's immediate post-YTS destinations, YTS cannot be described as a success story. Almost four in ten males (39 per cent) and three in ten females (29 per cent) were rewarded for their participation in YTS by a spell of unemployment on leaving. Just over a third of ex-trainees found immediate full-time employment with their YTS employer or sponsor (35 per cent of males and 34 per cent of females), while more than one in five young people (21 per cent of males and 26 per cent of females) entered full-time jobs immediately after YTS with a different employer (Furlong and Raffe, 1989). Training Agency figures present YTS in a slightly more favourable light by focusing on young people's destinations three months after they had left YTS. At this stage, some of those who were unemployed immediately after their schemes had found employment. Yet according to Training Agency figures (Training Agency, 1989d), around one in five young people were unemployed three months after leaving YTS, and around 15 per cent had gone on to join other schemes.

For those young people who were successful in moving directly from YTS into a job, the prospects were good , especially for young men. Furlong and Raffe (1989) report that more than eight out of every ten of those who moved straight into a job with their scheme employer or sponsor (92 per cent of males and 83 per cent of females) were still in full-time employment at the age of

19. Those who moved straight from YTS to a job with a different employer were slightly less likely to be in full-time employment at the age of 19 (76 per cent of males and 78 per cent of females).

Young people who did not enter full-time jobs straight after leaving YTS faced a particularly hard time in the labour market. Around four in ten of those who were unemployed straight after YTS were unemployed at the age of 19 (40 per cent of males and 42 per cent of females). Indeed, of those unemployed straight after YTS, only a third of males (33 per cent) and fewer than three in ten females (29 per cent) were in full-time jobs at the age of 19 (Furlong and Raffe, 1989). Obviously there are risks involved in joining YTS, yet it is difficult to provide an accurate measure of the 'effectiveness' of YTS as a route into the labour market because it is not easy to make an accurate assessment of the proportion of trainees who are guaranteed long-term jobs from the outset.

Focusing on minimum-age school-leavers who had not found employment immediately after leaving school, Main and Shelly (1988) try to assess the chances of trainees being employed a year later, comparing those who had joined YTS with those who had remained unemployed (removing from their analysis those who were subsequently employed by their YTS sponsor or employer). They produced a 'lower-bound' estimate of the effect of YTS on employment probability of just under 12 percentage points. Main (1990) repeated this analysis on the 1985 Scottish cohort and extended it to measure the effect on employment probability over a period of some three years after school leaving. This later analysis put the YTS 'effect' at between 14 and 19 percentage points. However, Main recognised that the increase in employment probability attributable to YTS was not sufficient to close the gap between 'advantaged' school-leavers who leave school with 'good' qualifications and live in areas of low unemployment, and 'disadvantaged' school-leavers with no qualifications and living in high unemployment areas (Main, 1990).

Research carried out in Ireland by Breen (1986) may help explain the advantages enjoyed by ex-trainees. Using multivariate analysis to assess the impact of the Irish Work Experience Programme, Breen has shown that job-seekers with work experience have increased prospects of finding employment. However, he argues that the scheme 'appears regressive in so far as it improves the chances of a job for those whose prospects are best to begin with, and therefore diminishes the chances of those who are most poorly placed' (Breen, 1986, p. 223). Although there is no evidence that the Youth Training Scheme has widened the gap between advantaged and disadvantaged school-leavers, there are similarities between schemes in Britain and Ireland; the best qualified are most likely to 'succeed' in the labour market after having been on the scheme (Chapter 5 and 8).

4.4 Attitudes to YTS

Much of the early work on young people's attitudes towards schemes stressed the hostility towards the allowance (which was not very much more than the supplementary benefit allowance) among young workers who were expected to put in a full week's work alongside other workers who were being paid the full rate for the job. Young people often regarded the Youth Opportunities Programme as 'slave labour' and resented the way employers could let ex-trainees go back on the dole at the end of their placement while substituting them with new trainees (Stafford, 1981; Ainley, 1986; Brown, 1987b). Furthermore, because YOP was introduced at a time of high youth unemployment, young people often regarded the scheme as an attempt by the Government to manipulate the unemployment figures. In the eyes of young people, it is difficult to justify why they should work for an employer who did not have to contribute towards their allowance, did not have to provide them with any training, and often made no commitment to the young person beyond the six-month duration of the scheme.

With the introduction of YTS, which included a compulsory element of off-the-job training, young people were getting something other than work experience for their efforts. However, attitudes towards schemes did not change overnight, and at first YTS was regarded in the same negative light as YOP (Seale, 1985; Raffe and Smith, 1987). Initially young people regarded YTS as an un-employment-based scheme (like YOP) and as a last resort for those who failed to find 'proper' jobs. Indeed, for many young people the differences between YOP and YTS were unclear (Kirkby and Roberts, 1984).

This view of schemes as alternatives to the dole tended to be reinforced in the school. Careers officers often suggested to young people that they first look for jobs, and should they not succeed, to 'come and see me about getting on a scheme' (Furlong, 1988a). In a study of young people in their final year of compulsory

66 *Growing up in a classless society*

schooling, most young people either felt that the careers officer was against them joining YTS, or wanted them to bear it in mind as an option in case they did not find a 'proper' job (Furlong, 1988a).

As YTS has become established, young people's attitudes towards it have become in general more favourable. Raffe and Smith (1987) and Raffe (1989b) have compared attitudes towards YTS among three different year groups: the first two year groups to become eligible to join YTS, and the fourth year group. Young people's attitudes were measured according to the strength of agreement or disagreement with five statements about YTS which were included in the Scottish Young People's Surveys: YTS 'helps unemployed young people to find jobs'; 'is a source of cheap labour'; gives people interesting things to do'; 'is just to keep un-employment figures down'; and 'is a useful way to get training'. Raffe and Smith (1987) reported a statistically significant decline in scores on this attitude scale between the first two year groups. Raffe (1989b) subsequently discovered a small but significant improvement in attitudes between the second and fourth year groups. Young people who experienced YTS themselves tended to be less hostile towards YTS than those with no experience of schemes. The attitudes towards YTS among those who found jobs after their schemes improved, while the attitudes of those who became unemployed afterwards deteriorated (Raffe, 1989b).

While aggregate measures of attitudes give some indication of the changes in the ways in which schemes are regarded by subsequent groups of school-leavers, the 'pervasive instrumentalism' that the first intakes felt towards schemes (Raffe and Smith, 1987) is still strongly in evidence. Among the fourth year group eligible for YTS, 70 per cent of young people felt that YTS was a 'source of cheap labour' and 61 per cent felt that its purpose was to 'keep the unemployment figures down' (Raffe, 1989b). However, Raffe reports that those who succeed in finding jobs after being on YTS are less likely to retain a belief that YTS is a source of cheap labour or is primarily to keep the unemployment figures down. Attitudes towards YTS are also affected by local labour market conditions. McDonald (1988) compared attitudes to YTS among young people in two contrasting labour markets: one with a long history of high levels of unemployment; the other a more prosperous one which had only recently experienced high levels of unemployment. He discovered that in the area which had a history of unemployment, young people's attitudes to YTS were negative, while in the more prosperous area, young people were more positive.

Young people often hold contradictory attitudes towards YTS: they have reservations about YTS as a scheme, but if they are unable to find acceptable jobs they will consider joining YTS. However, YTS is not simply used by young people as an alternative to the dole: they sometimes attempt to use schemes to their own advantage when they see schemes as offering them a chance to enter a skilled trade or occupation towards which they aspire (Ainley, 1986; Furlong, 1988a). Young people can regard schemes as 'slave labour', yet join as a method of trying to resist entering dead-end jobs (Brown, 1987b; Furlong, 1988a). This attitude is illustrated by a young woman in Leicester: 'Last year I'd have said I'm not going to go on a scheme, its just cheap labour. But when it came down to it, it was either do hairdressing on a scheme, or go in a shop or a factory. I still think it's slave labour, but it'll get me into hairdressing' (Furlong, 1987, p. 64). When young people use YTS as a method of trying to achieve their occupational aspirations, they become vulnerable later on should they fail to find the sorts of jobs for which they hoped YTS would open doors. While some young people may find that their aspirations are 'cooled-out' as a result of their scheme experience, other young people join schemes in order to try and maintain occupational aspirations they had been unable to realise in the labour market. If they are successful in maintaining earlier occupational aspirations while on YTS, they may face a crisis later on should they fail to achieve their aspirations (Furlong, 1987).

Those who have studied the role of schemes in the youth transition have often fallen into the trap of either seeing youth training schemes as semi-compulsory arrangements which exploit young people while providing few benefits for the majority of participants, or else they regard schemes as a genuine attempt on the part of the Training Agency (successful or not) to equip young people with the sorts of skills which will be to the advantage of themselves or their employers in the future. In reality, we need to locate YTS within the constraints of capitalist society in order to recognise that schemes can exploit young people *at the same time* as providing training and experience which will be beneficial to some young people (and their employers) when they try to re-enter the labour market. Furthermore, young people themselves are often aware of these contradictions: they know that employers are 'using' them, and they are often aware of the difference between schemes which lead nowhere and schemes which offer the possibility of gaining employment in a particular field. In other words, young people often try to use schemes as a way of *resisting* dead-end jobs, although others are able to exercise less choice and are forced on to schemes after having failed to secure a job or having been denied social security benefits.

4.5 Conclusion

Over the last decade, schemes have become a central part of the new 'protracted' transition from school to work. Yet routes from school to work remain highly stratified. Few of the best qualified school-leavers will experience YTS, and of those young people who do spend time on YTS, the sorts of schemes they join have implications for their future experiences in the labour market and their position in the social structure.

Some of the better qualified young people join YTS in preference to the 'proper' but dead-end jobs which are sometimes available in the local labour market, largely owing to the normative orientations which they have developed in the home and the school which make it important for them to enter 'respectable' or skilled jobs. However, while YTS has become a key route into a number of trades, it is unlikely to have a strong effect on the career chances of most trainees. Indeed, the evidence I have examined so far suggests that YTS may give young people a small advantage in the labour market, but the effect is not sufficient to close the gap between 'advantaged' and 'disadvantaged' school-leavers.

A particularly worrying feature of YTS is that it appears to create a group of young people who may become identified as 'double failures'. These are the young people who first fail to get a 'proper' job after leaving school and then fail to get a job straight after leaving YTS. The evidence suggests that they will find it particularly hard to obtain stable employment.

The negative attitudes young people held towards YOP eventually mellowed slightly; as YTS became established it managed to rid itself to some extent of its image as an unemployment-based scheme. However, while there are 'proper' jobs available, schemes are bound to be seen as second best to whatever sorts of jobs young people are hoping to enter (Lee *et al.*, 1990). Even in trades where entry is monopolised by YTS, young people are likely to wish they could return to the days in which school-leavers were able to enter 'proper' jobs for 'real' wages directly from school.

Notes

1. The MSC had its name changed to the Training Agency in 1989.
2. The number of young people being trained through apprentice-ships is likely to be under-represented as some employers use YTS to screen recruits for their apprentice training intake; formal apprenticeships may not begin until the end of the scheme. In addition, some apprentices will have been regarded as part of the permanent workforce and may have been unaware that they were on YTS.
3. The YTS leaving certificate is given to everyone who spends a minimum of twelve months on a scheme.
4. Young people taking Scotvec modules have more flexibility in this respect.

5

YOUTH UNEMPLOYMENT AND THE TRANSITION

5.1 Introduction

Before the 1980s youth unemployment tended to be associated either with a failure to make a successful entry into the world of work after leaving school or with voluntary job-changing and involuntary job-loss. In the new 'protracted' transition, the increasing number of possible routes into the labour market mean that young people become vulnerable to unemployment at a number of points in their post-school careers. With the introduction and expansion of youth schemes (combined with the removal of benefits from non-participants), a new pattern has emerged in which unemployment among people in their late teens has become more common as young people fail to find jobs after having been on schemes.

In Chapter 3 I discussed the trends in post-school unemployment over the decade to 1987 and argued that, largely because of schemes, the rise in unemployment among school-leavers remained relatively low. The prevalence of schemes meant that in the 1980s, many young people who experienced unemployment did so after having left schemes. There are close links between YTS and internal recruitment networks (Raffe, 1990), and employers may regard negatively those who are not retained by their scheme sponsors. Those who failed to find jobs after having been on YTS ran the risk of joining the long-term unemployed as they often encountered serious difficulties in finding jobs.

In this chapter I look first at some of the causes of the increase in youth unemployment and at the social and psychological effects of unemployment. Young people's chances of unemployment are strongly affected by the overall level of unemployment within a labour market, yet within an area we are able to make fairly reliable predictions about the groups who are most vulnerable to unemployment on the basis of their educational achievements, their personal and family characteristics and their prior labour market experiences. In the second part of the chapter, I attempt to identify the factors which increase individual vulnerability to unemployment and assess the extent to which we can predict vulnerability on the basis of such characteristics and experiences.

5.2 Causes of youth unemployment

Capitalist economies are subject to booms and slumps which affect the overall levels of employment within a society. Increases in levels of unemployment are often the consequence of downward cyclical shifts. When an economy goes into recession, as it did in Britain in the 1930s, the early 1980s and the early 1990s, the employment levels of both adults and young people decline. Levels of unemployment can also be affected by demographic trends, changes in the structure of employment opportunities and the economic strategies followed by the government of the day. In Britain, the policies which were being pursued by the Thatcher Government from 1979 and Major's Government from 1991 gave priority to reducing inflation and industrial 'overmanning'. Unemployment was regarded as a regrettable but largely unavoidable bi-product of deflationary policies. Although the Government was aware of the consequences of their economic and political decisions, the benefits of increased industrial efficiency were seen as outweighing the human costs of unemployment. Labour economists have tended to explain the recent increase in unemployment in terms of demand factors. Although there was lively debate about the nature of the causes of youth unemployment in the early 1980s, most commentators now agree that a fall in aggregate demand for labour was the most important factor (Makeham, 1980; Marsden, 1987; Junanker and Neale, 1987; Raffe, 1986b). In other words, unemployment rose due to a reduction in demand for labour caused by the recession.

Young people are more vulnerable to unemployment than adults. Makeham (1980) has estimated that a rise or fall of one percentage point in unemployment is associated with a corresponding rise or fall of 1·7 percentage points in the unemployment of young males and 3 percentage points in the unemployment of young females.[1] There are a number of reasons why young people do suffer disproportionately. School-leavers are more likely than adults to be seeking work in the first place, and anyone trying to enter the labour market at a time when employers are cutting back on recruitment are inevitably at a disadvantage. Young people have an additional problem in that they tend to be excluded from a wide range of jobs (Ashton *et al.*, 1982). Thurow (1975) has argued that young people are likely to be at the back of any job queue and tend to be hired only when there is a relatively high aggregate demand for labour. However, Thurow's 'job-queue' model has been criticised by labour market segmentation theorists who have argued that there are a number of job queues which correspond to different segments. While young people may tend to find themselves at the back of some queues, in others they may occupy an advantaged position (Hoskins *et al.*, 1989). Further, it has been suggested that, when employers make redundancies, young people are more likely than adults to lose their jobs as 'last-in, first-out' redundancy policies are often agreed with the unions (Ashton and Maguire, 1983). In addition, young people tend to display higher levels of job-changing than adults as they settle into the labour market (although in periods of high youth unemployment job-changing becomes less common). Lastly, young people tend to be concentrated in semi- and unskilled jobs which are characterised by high rates of labour turnover and as a result they are especially vulnerable to cyclical fluctuations (Ashton, 1986).

Although there is a general agreement that a fall in aggregate demand was one of the main causal factors in the increase in youth unemployment, some economists have argued that changes in the relative earnings of young people made them particularly vulnerable to unemployment in this period. Most economists accept that during the 1970s young people's earnings increased relative to adults. Where economists disagree is over the extent to which the rise in relative pay affected young people's ability to compete in the labour market and about the exact importance of relative wages in relation to the other factors which make young people vulnerable. Wells (1987) has argued strongly that young people's relative earnings had a powerful effect on their employment patterns during this period: 'The level of youth employment (especially for under 18-year-old males) is inversely related to changes in the relative labour costs and positively related to changes in the general level of demand for labour' (Wells, 1987, p. 52). However, other analysts have argued equally strongly that relative wages only had a marginal affect on unemployment levels. Junanker and Neale (1987) argued that 'the impact of relative wages on youth unemployment is often not significant and even when significant is quantitatively small' (p. 103). They argued that the rise in youth unemployment was almost wholly attributable to the decline in aggregate demand for labour and to structural changes in the economy. Other commentators have used data from different countries on the relative earnings of young people and have also concluded that there is no obvious link between the relative pay and relative unemployment of young people (Marsden, 1987).

Much of the controversy over the interpretation of the relationship between relative wages and youth unemployment has arisen because the available data is extremely poor. Given that all sides agree that the data must be interpreted with extreme care, the case for relative wage costs having made a worthwhile contribution to youth unemployment is at best unproven. It seems more plausible to regard the increase in relative wages and in youth unemployment in the 1970s as coincidental. Raffe (1986b) argues convincingly that in respect of young people, employers tend to see the hidden costs of supervision, control and training as of greater significance than relative wage costs.

Although there are few social scientists who do not accept that the fall in aggregate demand for labour was an important cause of the rise in unemployment, some have argued that there was a parallel process of structural change in the economy which had a powerful effect on youth unemployment. Ashton and Maguire (1983) and Jordan (1982), for example, regard increasing levels of youth unemployment as a consequence of a long-term process of change in the organisation of labour within capitalist economies. They regard high rates of youth unemployment as a permanent feature of the emerging society. Jordan (1982) argues for this hypothesis from a classical Marxist perspective and regards the decline in manufacturing industry as an inherent feature of capitalist society. He argues that capitalists are no longer able to increase profits by hiring additional labour and start to reduce their labour force as a way of increasing profitability. One of the problems with this approach is that it fails to take account of the expansion of the service sector as a provider of jobs (Braverman, 1974). It also fails to recognise the globalisation of capitalism through which manufacturing jobs are increasingly located in Third World countries which provide cheap labour, while western economies are increasingly characterised by dominant service sectors.

The approach taken by Ashton and Maguire (1983) emphasises

the changes which have taken place in the organisation of the labour market. They argue that the increase in youth unemployment was partly caused by a reduction in the number of 'points' at which young people were able to enter the labour market as employers started to recruit from different 'pools' of labour. For example, sales work increasingly became organised around part-time workers, and whereas employers previously recruited large numbers of young people for such jobs, they started to recruit more married women as they believed part-time vacancies to be unsuitable for young workers. The important point about this approach is that the changes in the labour market are not seen simply as the result of the recession, nor regarded as a consequence of 'forces' which are beyond the control of society, but are perceived as structural processes which are themselves a consequence of economic, social and political decisions.

Raffe (1986b) has criticised Ashton and Maguire for mistaking the effects of the recession, which are reversible, for long-term structural change, and has tried to show that there is no tendency for young people to be over-concentrated in declining industries. In turn, Ashton and colleagues (1990) have criticised Raffe for assuming that the labour market is relatively open, arguing that it is necessary to take account of the segmented nature of the youth labour market – especially of the differences between male and female labour markets. They argue that, for young males, the decline in the manufacturing sector and the growth of the service sector, together with the growth of part-time working and an increase in female participation in the labour market, have all led to a loss of jobs over and above that due to falling all-age unemployment; for females the loss was much smaller.

Employers' recruitment patterns may be changed according to the supply and demand for labour, and indeed, the forthcoming 'demographic timebomb' is likely to result in some radical changes in recruitment practices. Ironically, the Government's response to the increase in youth unemployment has itself led to the greatest structural change. The introduction of youth training schemes and the removal of social security benefits from young people has led to a situation where the youth labour market has largely been replaced by a 'surrogate labour market' (Lee *et al.*, 1990). A large proportion of school-leavers now spend their first two years in the labour market on schemes which are largely financed by the Government.

5.3 *The Consequences of youth unemployment*

In a period when unemployment has become a 'normal' part of the transition from school to work, there is a temptation to trivialise the consequences of unemployment for those who experience it. A cursory look at the literature demonstrates that the experience of unemployment has serious consequences. Much of the psychological work on unemployment was undertaken in periods of high unemployment, especially in the 1930s (e.g. Pilgrim Trust, 1938; Eisenberg and Lazarsfeld, 1938; Bakke, 1933) and in the 1980s (e.g. Warr, 1987; Banks and Ullah, 1988; Jahoda, 1987). Many people experienced unemployment in both these periods, and the evidence has consistently highlighted the suffering it causes.

The psychological effects of unemployment on individuals is often described in terms of a cycle in which people suffer initially yet eventually learn to cope with the effects of having lost their jobs and adjust to the loss of status and to their lower standard of living. Eisenberg and Lazarsfeld (1938) argued that on becoming unemployed the person would first experience shock, but this first phase was closely followed by a second phase in which the individual starts to seek employment and remains optimistic about their chances of finding work. Eventually the individual loses this optimism and enters a third phase in which they become depressed, having given up hope of finding an early end to their unemployment. In the final stage of this model, the individual becomes fatalistic and starts to adapt to being unemployed.

Since this model was developed, others have tried to refine and extend it, but later models still tend to follow the broad outline put forward by Eisenberg and Lazarsfeld. Hopson and Adams (1976), for example, developed an extended model in which the individual first experiences 'immobilisation', which is a state of shock and disbelief. Second they enter the 'minimisation' stage in which they continue to act as if they had not become unemployed. The third stage is characterised by depression as they come to appreciate the extent of the changes that will have to be made. After the depression stage comes the first of four stages in which the individual comes to terms with changing circumstances. For this to happen, they must accept the changed reality and let go of their past assumptions and expectations. They then test out the new reality and experiment with new ways of coping. Following this, they start to search for meaning within the changed reality and eventually internalise these new meanings.

One of the criticisms which has been levelled against the psychological stage model is that work tends to be equated with paid employment. Consequently psychologists often make generalisations which are based on the ways in which middle-aged males experience unemployment and this may not be appropriate for other groups of workers (Ashton, 1986). Ashton suggests that, because of this shortcoming, the model is unable to distinguish the effects of job-loss from the effects of loss of income. 'The loss of income and of control over resources which that implies is one of the major problems facing the unemployed. Yet these problems are of a different order from those which stem from the threat unemployment makes to a person's identity' (Ashton, 1986, p. 143).

There are important differences between the ways in which adults and young people experience unemployment. It seems to be true, for example, that the levels of stress and the reduction in psychological well-being among young people are not as great as for middle-aged people with financial or family responsibilities. In some parts of the country, young people may even anticipate spending some time out of work after leaving school. As far as young people are concerned, the psychological stage model was not designed to account for the experiences of school-leavers for whom unemployment prior to job entry is common. For young people it is often inappropriate to talk of job 'loss'. However, young people do experience a reduction in psychological well-being on becoming unemployed, which suggests that those who become unemployed are having to deal with a difficult event (Furlong and Spearman, 1989). Studies of young people who are unemployed have tended to find that they suffer from reduced levels of well-being and self-esteem when compared to their counterparts in jobs or in education (Banks and Ullah, 1988; Furlong and Spearman, 1989). But current evidence suggests that psychological well-being does not deteriorate with length of unemployment (Banks and Ullah, 1988; Furlong and Spearman, 1989) and that the effect of the reduction in psychological well-being is hard to detect once a young person has secured work (Furlong and Spearman, 1989).

While there are some differences between the ways young people and adults experience unemployment, there are many similarities. Becoming unemployed involves a rapid increase in the time available for 'leisure' activities. For adults this enforced 'leisure' is often utilised, at first, as the unemployed worker catches up with neglected household tasks, such as painting the house or tidying up the garden (Hill, 1978). Consequently the loss of daily structure may not be felt for some weeks. Similarly, for young people, the initial weeks after the end of school are often treated as an extended holiday (Hendry, *et al.*, 1984). Friends who have jobs to go to may well not start until the end of the summer vacation, and the loss of the daily structure imposed by the school is replaced by 'summer holiday' leisure.

Not only are young people from working-class homes more prone to unemployment than their middle-class counterparts, it has been suggested that those from working-class homes have less trouble filling the time provided by unemployment than their middle-class peers (Ashton, 1986; Willis, 1977). In a study of young people in Leicester (Furlong, 1988a) it was suggested that differences in the social lives of the young unemployed are closely related to class, gender and the structure of the local community. On a large council estate which was characterised by high levels of unemployment, young people who were unemployed tended to have fairly active social lives, especially the males. They tended to utilise some of the facilities for the unemployed on the estate: the Recreation Centre if they liked sports, or the Unemployed Drop-in Centre (known locally as the 'Cabbage Club') if they preferred something less energetic. Everyone's day included a fairly large element of social activity which tended to reach a climax 'on an evening' when other friends who had jobs in the day were free (Furlong, 1988a). Conversely, young people living in middle-class areas tended to be much more isolated in their unemployment and engaged in fewer activities. They were more likely to spend whole mornings in bed and to watch TV for much of the afternoon and evening.

Banks and Ullah (1988) have suggested that unemployed young people are relatively isolated from their employed peers even at times when the employed have finished work. While this may be true in more middle-class areas, on the council estate studied by Furlong (1988a) the social interaction of the employed and unemployed continued. The crucial factor here was whether or not they lived on the estate. Boys who did not live on the estate often lived in areas with low levels of unemployment and did not have friends nearby who were out of work. In areas where unemployment is low, the unemployed tend to be more stigmatised

(Banks and Ullah, 1988) and this can aggravate the isolation of the unemployed. In both areas the young women were less likely to engage in activities outside the home and were often expected to do the housework or look after the children of a working relative (see also Hendry *et al.*, 1984; Millham *et al.*, 1978; Pahl, 1978). For many unemployed young women, their main social activity was having their boyfriend visit during the evening.

In order to fully understand the ways in which unemployment affects the lives of young people, it is necessary to go beyond descriptions of social deprivation and models which describe the psychological 'stages' of unemployment (with implicit implications of uniform experiences of unemployment) towards a greater understanding of the ways in which unemployment affects young people's self-perceptions. Throughout their socialisation children are taught about the importance of work and come to realise that their future occupations will form the basis of their identity and future status (Hayes and Nutman, 1981). Young people's orientations towards work are of crucial importance, in that for some, work is seen as a central area of achievement, a means through which to implement their occupational self-concept, while for others satisfaction comes not from work itself but from the material rewards of work (Ashton and Field, 1976) as well as from the status of becoming a worker (Willis, 1977).

Young people's normative orientations in relation to work are central to an understanding of the ways in which they experience unemployment. Unemployment is distressing for most young people, but for different reasons. For those young people for whom work is peripheral to their overall self-concept, the absence of a wage and the failure to achieve the status of wage-earner can cause most concern. In contrast, the young people for whom work is central to their overall self-concept may be distressed because their self-image as a person capable of securing white-collar work or an apprenticeship is being challenged (Jackson *et al.*, 1983; Furlong, 1987).

Indeed, while young people remain confident about fulfilling earlier aspirations, they will often avoid taking jobs which they regard as inferior (Roberts *et al.*, 1982; Jones, 1983; Furlong, 1988a). In a study of Birmingham school-leavers, for example, Jones (1983) discovered that that those young people with the greatest confidence in obtaining the sort of job they wanted tended to persist in their attempts to find that job, whilst those with lower levels of confidence were more likely to accept the less desirable alternative (see also MacKay and Reid, 1972).

It is in this context that some youth unemployment has been characterised as self-inflicted (Roberts *et al.*, 1982); as some young-sters prefer to remain unemployed and retain their previous aspir-ations, rather than enter unskilled jobs when they feel them-selves to be capable of better. However, experiences within a local labour market characterised by high levels of youth unemploy-ment will eventually 'cool-out' (Goffman, 1952) young peoples aspirations. Unemployed young people tend not to have unrealis-tically high aspirations, and eventually most will accept any job they can get (Furlong, 1988a). As Seabrook has argued,

> one of the great advantages to capitalism of the present high level of unemployment, with the sense of futility that attends it, is that it prepares people to accept any kind of work, because anything is better than staying idle. Jobs in themselves come to seem desirable, no matter what indignities their creation heaps upon people, no matter how demeaning they are. The young who have never had a job come to feel it is a privilege to do anything (Seabrook, 1982, p. 104).

While unemployment 'cools-out' young people's aspirations, Sea-brook tends to exaggerate the eagerness with which young people take up menial jobs and underplays their resentment at having to do so. Unemployment may make young people more willing to accept jobs they once considered to be beneath them, but others continue to hold out for the jobs they originally desired, or whilst accepting other jobs, regard them as being temporary. These young people are concerned not simply about the prospect of continued unemployment, but also about the quality of jobs they are offered (Coffield, et al., 1983; Furlong, 1987).

5.4 Characteristics of the young unemployed

So far in this chapter, I have looked at some of the causes of youth unemployment in Britain and have examined some of the effects of unemployment on young people. However, much of the work on the effects of unemployment addresses the issue from an indi-vidualistic perspective. Unemployment is also a social rather than merely an individual phenomenon. C. Wright Mills makes this important point when he says that:

> When in a city of 100,000, only one man is unemployed, that is his personal trouble, and for its relief we properly look to

the characteristics of the man, his skills, and his immediate opportunities. But when in a nation of 50 million employees, 15 million men are unemployed, that is an issue, and we may not hope to find its solution within the range of opportunities open to any one individual. The very structure of opportunities has collapsed. Both the correct statement of the problem and the range of possible solutions require us to consider the economic and political institutions of the society, and not merely the personal situation and character of a scatter of individuals (Mills, 1968, p 9).

In capitalist society one's position in the class structure has a powerful effect on life chances. Young people's achievements and their future position in the social structure are strongly affected by their social class of origin through the mediating role of education. Social disadvantage is translated into educational disadvantage and young people who fail to achieve in educational terms tend to be disadvantaged in the labour market. Of course there are exceptions: some young people from lower working-class families 'make good' through their educational performance and achieve high levels of social mobility. Other young people from privileged backgrounds become downwardly mobile as a result of 'failing' in the educational system. These exceptions are important because they give people the impression that occupational mobility is dependent on one's own efforts; those from disadvantaged backgrounds who succeed are held up as 'proof' that anyone can achieve great things if they have the ability and if they make the effort.

In Chapter 2 I argued that despite meritocratic ideals, young people's educational achievements continue to be strongly influenced by social class. Young people from working-class families tend to leave school with fewer qualifications than those from more advantaged class backgrounds and are ultimately placed in positions where they are vulnerable to unemployment and labour market disadvantage. Over the decade 1977 to 1987 those with fewest qualifications became increasingly 'at risk' of unemployment. Although I found no evidence to support the hypothesis that those from disadvantaged class positions *increased* their vulnerability to long-term unemployment over the decade once I controlled for qualifications, there were important shortcomings in my analysis. The information presented in Chapter 3 was that the best information on young people's destinations over the decade only covered young people up to ten months after the majority had left school. By the mid-1980s many of those who experienced unemployment during their transition from school to work did so after finishing YTS.

In order to arrive at a fuller, more accurate, picture of youth unemployment in the mid-1980s, information from the cohort of Scottish young people who became eligible to leave education in 1984 can now be used in order to examine the experiences of this year group over a two-and-a-half year period. During the 1980s unemployment became a part òf the transitional experience for many young people. In autumn 1987 when the average age of members of the cohort was 19·25, 16 per cent of the year group described themselves as 'unemployed and looking for work', while a further 4 per cent were on schemes for the unemployed. However, just over half (53 per cent) had had some experience of unemployment since leaving school.

The unemployment rate among the cohort had increased from 5 per cent in autumn 1984 to a peak of 18 per cent in spring 1986. Male unemployment was higher than female unemployment at each point: for males, unemployment peaked at 20 per cent, while for females it peaked at 16 per cent. For most young people the experience of unemployment occurred some time after leaving school. The majority of the cohort had left school by spring 1985 (57 per cent), but the unemployment rate in the group remained relatively low until autumn 1985 when those who had joined the Youth Training Scheme after finishing fourth year began to re-enter the labour market.

Not only did the unemployment rate increase as the year-group got older, but the length of time young people spent out of work also increased as they found it more difficult to find jobs. At each time point, a large proportion of those who were unemployed had been unemployed six months earlier (Table 5.1). In spring 1985, just over a third of respondents who had reported themselves as unemployed (36 per cent) had been unemployed six months previously. Between spring 1985 and spring 1987, the proportion of young people who had been unemployed six months earlier steadily increased. By spring 1986, a majority of those who were unemployed had been unemployed six months earlier (56 per cent), while by spring 1987 more than two in three (70 per cent) had been unemployed six months previously. This pattern was similar for males and females.

TABLE 5.1 Status of young people six months prior to reporting themselves as unemployed (%)

Status six months earlier	Unemployed			School			YTS			Other scheme			Job			FT FE/HE			Other			Total	Unweighted n		
	M	F	A	M	F	A	M	F	A	M	F	A	M	F	A	M	F	A	M	F	A	A	M	F	A
Date of employment																									
Spring 1985	35	37	36	31	25	28	23	17	20	0	0	0	7	13	10	1	3	2	4	4	4	100	(170)	(133)	(303)
Autumn 1985	42	40	41	4	11	7	39	29	35	0	0	0	9	12	10	1	4	3	5	4	4	100	(239)	(201)	(440)
Spring 1986	56	55	56	2	2	2	25	18	22	0	0	0	13	17	15	1	2	2	2	6	4	101	(296)	(234)	(530)
Autumn 1986	62	57	60	5	9	7	8	9	9	0	0	0	17	11	14	3	8	5	4	6	5	100	(278)	(251)	(529)
Spring 1987	69	70	70	0	0	0	1	3	2	8	3	6	15	21	18	3	2	3	3	2	2	101	(272)	(231)	(503)
Autumn 1987	57	57	57	0	0	0	2	0	1	14	4	10	18	18	18	6	13	9	3	6	4	99	(260)	(227)	(487)

M=Male F=Female A=All

TABLE 5.2 Destinations of young people six months after having reported themselves as unemployed (%)

Status six months earlier / Date of unemployment	Unemployed M F A	Job M F A	YTS M F A	Other scheme M F A	FT FE/HE M F A	Other M F A	Total M	Unweighted n M F A
Autumn 1984	57 56 56	17 10 14	26 28 27	0 0 0	0 3 1	0 3 2	100	(104) (82) (186)
Spring 1985	56 57 57	18 20 19	17 10 14	0 0 0	3 3 3	7 10 8	101	(170) (133) (303)
Autumn 1985	69 65 67	19 19 19	5 6 6	0 0 0	0 1 0	6 9 7	99	(239) (201) (440)
Spring 1986	56 56 56	21 22 22	2 1 2	12 4 9	3 3 3	5 14 8	100	(296) (234) (530)
Autumn 1986	67 66 67	15 18 16	0 1 0	15 6 11	0 1 1	2 8 5	100	(278) (251) (529)
Spring 1987	54 55 54	20 22 21	0 0 0	18 7 11	4 6 5	3 11 7	98	(272) (231) (503)

M=Male F=Female A=All

Throughout the period covered by the survey, the proportion of the year-group who became unemployed after having been in full-time employment was relatively small as most young people became unemployed after leaving school or YTS. Once unemployed, it was difficult to escape; a majority of those who were unemployed at any one time point were still unemployed six months later (Table 5.2). Indeed, in none of the six-month periods covered by the survey did more than 22 per cent of unemployed young people of either sex make the transition from unemployment to full-time employment. Furthermore, of those who did manage to leave the ranks of the unemployed, few entered full-time jobs directly and many only avoided continued unemployment by joining YTS or other schemes such as the Job Training Scheme (JTS) and the Community Programme (CP). Those who ended their unemployment by joining schemes were at risk of further unemployment on completing their schemes.

To the extent that young people find it difficult to escape from unemployment, we can argue that unemployment careers are firmly established at a young age. It is certainly true that those who reported themselves as unemployed in autumn 1987 tended to have had much greater experience of unemployment than those who were in jobs or education at the time. In a survey of unemployed young people between the ages of 18 and 24 who had been unemployed for six months or more, White and McRae (1989) discovered that about a quarter had never had a job. Indeed, they argued that the absence of any employment record put these young people at an extra disadvantage.

Among the Scottish cohort, those who were unemployed had spent a mean total of 73 weeks unemployed since school (males 76 weeks, females 69 weeks), while those who were working in autumn 1987 had spent a mean total of 12 weeks unemployed (males 13 weeks, females 12 weeks) and those in education a mean total of 2 weeks unemployed (males 3 weeks, females 2 weeks). Over half (56 per cent) of those unemployed in autumn 1987 reported that their longest period was in excess of a year (55 per cent of males, 57 per cent of females). Only 13 per cent of those in jobs and 9 per cent of those in education reported a period of unemployment of more than a year. These figures lead us to suggest that a large proportion of those young people who were unemployed at the age of 19 were not 'between jobs' but were young people who had substantially greater experiences of unemployment than those who were in jobs. Many of these un-employed young people appear to have become trapped in a cycle of unemployment and unemployment-based schemes from which they were finding it increasingly difficult to escape (see also Ashton *et al.*, 1990).

Harris (1987) identified a similar pattern among adult workers in South Wales who followed a 'chequered' career pattern involv-ing regular movements between schemes, unemployment and semi- and unskilled jobs. While this pattern was once common only among a section of the unskilled working class (Norris, 1978), Ashton and colleagues (1990) have argued that this is be-coming a normal pattern of work experience for a large propor-tion of the working class. The evidence presented here suggests that chequered career patterns are established at an early age.

As it is clear that the labour market experiences of unemployed 19-year-olds tend to be different from the experiences of many of those in more secure segments of the labour market, it is impor-tant to examine their social and educational backgrounds in order to achieve a greater understanding of which young people are most vulnerable to the sorts of labour market experiences which lead to unemployment in young adults. Literature on youth un-employment has consistently shown that socially and education-ally disadvantaged young people tend to experience a dispropor-tionate share of unemployment (Ashton *et al.*, 1982; Gray *et al.*, 1983; Furlong and Raffe, 1989; White and McRae, 1989). The un-employed were less likely than thcse in jobs or in education to have come from the professional and managerial classes and were more likely to have had fathers who were unemployed or unable to work. While 21 per cent of those who were working and 55 per cent of those who continued their education were from profes-sional and managerial classes, only 10 per cent of the unemployed were from these classes. Similarly, 12 per cent of those working and 6 per cent of those who continued their education described their fathers as unemployed or unable to work, while 28 per cent of those who were unemployed at the age of 19 said that their fathers were unemployed or unable to work. In other words, of the 16 per cent of the cohort who were unemployed in autumn 1987, just over one in four had a father who was unemployed or unable to work. In contrast, of those who were in full-time jobs, just over one in ten had a father who was reported as unemployed or unable to work.

Using data from the 1980 and 1981 General Household Surveys, Payne (1987) has shown that young people who are unemployed are far more likely than than those in jobs to have another member of their family out of work. As working family members may be a useful source of knowledge of unadvertised job vacancies (Manwaring, 1984), family unemployment may cut a young person off from an important information network. The social disadvantages of the unemployed have been emphasised in many studies. Family experience of unemployment has a strong influence on the employment chances of the young person, as does coming from a large family, coming from a single parent family and belonging to an ethnic minority (White and McRae, 1989). However, the young adults who were unemployed in autumn 1987 were disadvantaged educationally in comparison to those who were working or in full-time education. In terms of qualifications, those who were unemployed had a mean total of 1·3 O grade passes, compared with a mean total of 2·8 O grades among those in jobs and 6·9 O grades among those who had continued in education. Within each status category, females tended to have a greater number of O grade passes than males. However, White and McRae (1989) argue that it is wrong to depict the unemployed as an 'unqualified residue in the labour market' as they tend to have similar qualifications to those working in low-skilled occupations. In other words, unskilled workers are particularly vulnerable to unemployment and can be seen as following a chequered career pattern. Indeed, Ashton and colleagues (1986) found a tendency for the young unemployed to be better qualified than those in unskilled jobs; some of those who are out of work are qualified to enter skilled and white-collar positions in the labour market.

The argument that unskilled workers are particularly vulnerable to unemployment is supported by evidence from the Scottish cohort. Among those who were unemployed in autumn 1987, 63 per cent (55 per cent of males and 72 per cent of females) of those working full-time in spring 1986 had been employed in relatively low-skilled occupations: sales, personal service, operatives and labourers. Among the cohort as a whole, 49 per cent (44 per cent of males and 54 per cent of females) of those who were working were employed in one of these three occupations. The argument that young people with few educational achievements, those from disadvantaged social backgrounds and those with a history of unemployment are particularly vulnerable to unemployment is supported by a large body of recent literature (Raffe, 1984a; Ashton *et al.*, 1986 and 1990; Roberts *et al.*, 1986; Furlong and Raffe, 1989). Yet in any analysis which identifies characteristics of the unemployed, it is important to remember that those possessing certain characteristics only become vulnerable to unemployment under specific economic circumstances. Unemployment is caused by a lack of demand for labour rather than by inadequacies in the labour force. Those who are unemployed in a recession are perfectly acceptable to employers when labour demand is high.

In the early 1980s, there was a disequilibrium in the supply and demand for jobs for young people (Wells, 1987) in many local labour markets across Britain. However, in some local labour markets the gap between the supply and demand for jobs for young people was far larger than in other areas. In those areas were the gap was largest, highly qualified young people from relatively advantaged social backgrounds were finding it difficult to get jobs. In Sunderland, for example, even those with A levels had problems finding work, while in areas with low unemployment, such as St Albans, relatively few qualified school-leavers were unemployed for any length of time (Ashton *et al.*, 1986). Employers faced with increasing numbers of applicants for a reduced number of vacancies tend not to make radical changes in their recruitment practices, but accentuate existing practices (Manwaring and Wood, 1984). In other words, they make greater use of informal networks, recruit experienced workers rather than school-leavers, and when they do recruit young people, they are able to choose from among the better qualified.

In the mid-1980s, as youth unemployment rates started to fall, young workers were in short supply in some local labour markets, particularly in the South East of England. However, in other local labour markets, such as those in the North of England and in the West of Scotland, young people were still having difficulties in finding jobs. The characteristics of local labour markets are important to any analysis of the ways in which young people are made vulnerable to unemployment, yet in a theoretical sense we know little about the relationship between area characteristics and the social and educational characteristics of the inhabitants of an area. In the following section, I will attempt to assess the relative influences of each of these factors on the probability of being unemployed (or on unemployment-based schemes) in autumn 1987.

5.5 Unemployment probability

In order to examine the strength of the various factors which affect the probability of young people being unemployed, it is necessary to clarify the relative strength of different aspects of the local labour market. Local area factors like the level of unemployment have been shown to affect young people's experiences (Ashton *et al.*, 1988; Garner *et al.*, 1988) and young people who live in areas with above-average rates of all-age unemployment tend to have restricted opportunities. Areas with above-average rates of unemployment tend to be areas with a concentration of declining industries in which employment opportunities are often skewed towards manual workers.

Other features of the local labour market such as the proportion of young people who experience YTS and the proportion of minimum-age school-leavers in an area tend not to have been discussed, yet both of these factors could be expected to affect young people's chances of unemployment. In areas with a shortage of jobs for young people, we would expect to find a high proportion of young people experiencing YTS. A high proportion of minimum-age school-leavers in an area could be indicative either of an area with below-average socio-economic composition, or an area in which the sorts of opportunities in the youth labour market were mainly geared towards minimum-age school-leavers.

I used multivariate analysis to assess the significance of the different aspects of local opportunity structures in predicting the total number of weeks young people had been unemployed by autumn 1987 among young people who had entered the labour market by spring 1985 and were still in the labour market.[2] The analysis confirmed that school qualifications were important in helping young people to avoid unemployment. Those with O grades tended to have less experience of unemployment, although the number of O grades young people gained was relatively unimportant. Young men with vocational qualifications or Scotvec modules also tended to experience less unemployment although the effect on females was not as great. However, as more males take vocational qualifications whilst in jobs, the apparent effect of vocational qualifications may in part reflect the fact that these young men had found (good) jobs on leaving school. In contrast, females were more likely to take vocational qualifications prior to starting work.

The experience of YTS appears to have had little effect on total unemployment among females, while for males experience of YTS was associated with an increase in time spent unemployed. This does not necessarily imply that YTS was the cause of their extended unemployment, as many young people will have joined YTS because they were unable to find jobs. When area level predictors were added to the model, the effect of YTS on unemployment experience became insignificant suggesting that the association between YTS participation and unemployment is a consequence of high levels of YTS recruitment in high unemployment areas. The association between social background and unemployment was also evident Those who had unemployed fathers tended to experience more unemployment than those whose fathers were employed. Fathers' occupations also affected the time spent unemployed: young people with fathers whose occupations received high ratings on the Cambridge occupational status scale[3] tended to have less experience of unemployment than those with fathers in low-status occupations.

If we look at the influence of local factors, it is clear that the local all-age unemployment rate tends to be the best predictor of total unemployment among young people. In areas of high unemployment young people tended to have spent a greater proportion of their time since school unemployed. These effects were stronger and more significant for males than females; this is likely to be a consequence of an expanding service sector and declining manufacturing sector which advantages females in terms of employment (Ashton *et al.*, 1990). When other local area predictors were included in the model, the effect of the local all-age unemployment rate was weakened considerably. In part, this is because some of the other area-level predictors also reflect the incidence of unemployment.

When variables measuring total experience of YTS within a Travel to Work Area (TTWA) and the proportion of minimum-age school-leavers within a TTWA were added to the model, there was a strong decline in the predictive value of the local unemployment rate. Although the total experience of YTS in a TTWA tended to be a good predictor of male unemployment, this may be regarded as a proxy for local unemployment rates (perhaps more sensitive to the youth unemployment rate than the global, all-age measure). The occupational structure of the area did not have a significant effect on total unemployment,[4] although females who lived in areas in which a high proportion of the workforce were employed in service industries tended to experience more unemployment. This conceivably reflects the dominance of a 'secondary' labour market offering relatively unstable, temporary jobs, but such inferences are at best conjecture.

The multivariate model demonstrated an association between participation on YTS and an increase in total unemployment (significant for males but not for females), so the relationship between unemployment and YTS merits further investigation. Although the majority of those who were unemployed at the age of 19 had experienced YTS (62 per cent), less than three in ten of those who had been on YTS were unemployed at this stage. Males with experience of YTS were more likely than females to be unemployed in autumn 1987.

If we are to judge the effect of YTS participation on unemployment, it is important to have some measure of the effect of non-participation. However, it is difficult to assess whether those who refused a place on YTS increased their vulnerability to unemployment as it is not possible to identify 'refusers' accurately from the Scottish Young People's Survey. In the 1985 survey, young people were asked, 'Have you ever turned down the offer of a place on the Youth Training Scheme?', and in the 1986 survey they were asked, 'Have you ever been offered a place on the Youth Training Scheme?'. The problem arises because some young people may have refused a YTS as they wanted a different sort of placement, while others may have refused as they had an offer of a job or a place on a course or were expecting to be made an offer. Similarly, some of those who had not been on YTS but said that they had been offered a place may have had jobs to go to, while others may not have put themselves forward for a place. In addition there is the problem that some young people may have avoided being made an offer by deliberately 'messing up' interviews.

If we adopt a strict definition of YTS refusal, classing refusers as young people who had never been on YTS yet reported themselves as unemployed at the first 'snapshot' date after leaving school (autumn 1984 for those who left from the fourth year, and spring 1985 for those who left at Christmas of the fifth year) and also either stated they had been offered a YTS place (yet not taken it up) or that they had refused a YTS place, some 3 per cent of the cohort could be classed as 'refusers'. On the other hand, if we take a more liberal definition, classing refusers as young people who

TABLE 5.3 Unemployment[+] in autumn 1987 by YTS
participation, completion and post-YTS destination (%)

	Unemployment Rate			Unweightedn (base)		
	All	Male	Female	All	Male	Female
Experience of YTS	28	32	23	(1391)	(736)	(655)
Refused YTS (liberal definition)	55	66	39	(140)	(84)	(56)
Completed YTS, full-time job after	13	11	16	(429)	(251)	(178)
Completed YTS, unemployed after	52	57	43	(255)	(160)	(95)
Completed YTS, neither full-time job nor unemployed after	23	29	20	(54)	(22)	(32)
YTS not completed, full-time job after	9	12	7	(364)	(145)	(219)
YTS not completed, unemployed after	61	67	53	(141)	(81)	(60)
YTS not completed, neither full-time job nor unemployment after	25	(34)	22	(52)	(16)	(36)

Notes: 1. Brackets denote base n of less than 20.
2 . + Includes respondents on unemployment-based schemes such as CP & JTS.

had never been on YTS but who were unemployed at the first 'snapshot' date after leaving school, 5 per cent of the cohort could be classed as refusers. The liberal definition is used in Table 5.3. In both approaches, we face the problem of distinguishing the effect of YTS refusal and the effect of an early period of unemployment on a later period of unemployment. In the more liberal approach we must recognise that some 'refusers' may not have been made an offer to refuse. Despite these problems, adopting a strict or liberal definition of YTS refusal makes little difference to the proportion of refusers who were unemployed in autumn 1987. Using the strict definition, 58 per cent were unemployed, and using the liberal definition 55 per cent were unemployed. Males who refused YTS were more likely than females to be unemployed in autumn 1987.

The unemployment rate in autumn 1987 among those who had experienced YTS was lower than among those who had refused a place. However, immediate post-YTS destinations and having stayed on YTS until the end of the scheme both affected subsequent unemployment. Among those who moved straight from YTS to full-time jobs, relatively few were unemployed in autumn 1987: for males it made little difference whether or not they completed their schemes, while females who completed YTS were more likely to be unemployed than those who left early. Those who were unemployed immediately after their schemes were less likely to have been unemployed in autumn 1987 if they had completed their schemes.

The relationship between YTS participation, completion and unemployment is obviously complex. On the face of it, it would seem that immediate post-YTS destinations are at least as important as completion. Yet unemployment among 19-year-olds may be explained more accurately by young people's social and educational characteristics than by their experiences of YTS. In order to assess the effect of YTS on the likelihood of unemployment in autumn 1987 it was necessary to measure the strength of the other factors which affected young people's chances of unemployment. To do this, I constructed a logit model to assess the relative chances of being unemployed (or on unemployment-based schemes) in autumn 1987 among minimum-age leavers with different post-school experiences.[5] As YTS was aimed principally at those who left school at the earliest opportunity, the model is restricted to those who left school at the end of the fourth year or at Christmas of the fifth year.

The most important conclusion to emerge from the logit model is that personal experience of unemployment (after leaving school or after YTS) or having an unemployed father has a powerful effect on subsequent chances of unemployment which is not fully countered by YTS participation. The relative chances of unemployment among males who were unemployed in the autumn or spring after leaving school were almost twice that of those who were not unemployed on those occasions, while for females relative chances increased by 60 percentage points. Males who were unemployed immediately after YTS had their chances of unemployment at age 19 increased by 60 percentage points, while females saw their chances increase by 70 percentage points.

Those who had fathers who were unemployed were also at a high risk of personal unemployment. Males with unemployed fathers were more likely to be unemployed at age 19 than those whose fathers were not unemployed by some 60 percentage points, while females were more likely to be unemployed by 50 percentage points. The chances of personal unemployment and family unemployment were both influenced by the level of employment within the local labour market. The local unemployment rate in October 1987 had a significant effect on the chances of unemployment among males, but not among females. Although father's unemployment was important in predicting unemployment among young people, father's occupation did not have a significant effect. However, the effect of father's occupation on chances of unemployment may have been mediated by educational achievements and by the variable measuring post-school unemployment. For young people who left school at the earliest opportunity, school qualifications were more important in reducing the chances of unemployment among males than females. Relative to those who did not sit any SCE examinations, young people with O grade passes were less likely to be unemployed.

Males and females with experience of YTS reduced their chances of being unemployed in autumn 1987 by around 20 percentage points. However those young people who were unemployed immediately after YTS had their chances of being unemployed in autumn 1987 substantially increased. In sum, it appears that YTS experience payoff in terms of reducing young people's chances of unemployment, although due to the association between post-YTS unemployment and later experience of unemployment, it would not be worthwhile joining a scheme if there was little chance of subsequent employment.

5.6 Conclusion

Despite the increase in the number of routes young people are able to follow after the age of 16, those who are socially or educationally disadvantaged remain particularly vulnerable to unemployment when demand is low, especially if they have a father who is unemployed or if they live in an area of high unemployment. Unemployment is difficult to escape from, and once a young person becomes unemployed it can be difficult to get a foothold in the job market.

Since the introduction of YTS, a greater proportion of school-leavers have undergone formal post-school training at colleges and training centres, yet this has not led to a more open opportunity structure for minimum-age school-leavers. Those young people who were disadvantaged prior to joining YTS were most likely to experience unemployment after YTS. These young people may then have an additional stigma resulting from a failure to secure employment after YTS. Many of those who become unemployed after YTS will not leave the unemployment register through gaining 'ordinary' employment, but will leave to join unemployment-based schemes. For many young people, YTS is a gamble. Joining a scheme may pay dividends in terms of a job at the end, but should they fail to hit the jackpot, then they may even have increased their chances of unemployment in the long-term.

Notes

1. In part, the apparent greater vulnerability of young females is a consequence of the failure of official statistics to accurately measure fluctuations in female unemployment (Makeham, 1980).
2. Details of the regression model are provided in Appendix II.
3. The Cambridge Status Scale used in this analysis is an updated version of the scale originally described by Stewart, Prandy and Blackburn (1980) which was kindly made available by Ken Prandy. It has been described in a recent article by Prandy (1990).
4. In a separate analysis the BROADWOC categories were added one at a time and this failed to produce statistically significant results.
5. Details of the logit model are provided in Appendix II.

6

LABOUR MARKET WITHDRAWAL, UNEMPLOYMENT
AND WORK ETHICS

6.1 Labour market withdrawal

In Chapter 5 I argued that despite an increase in the range of education and training options which are open to young people, those from disadvantaged families, those living in areas of high unemployment and those with few school-leaving qualifications remain particularly vulnerable to unemployment and that failure to secure a job immediately after having been on YTS may increase one's chances of long-term unemployment. While unemployed young people have been the focus of a number of studies, those who withdraw from the labour market tend to be less visible. In this chapter I first examine the extent to which 19-year-olds in the Scottish cohort had withdrawn from the labour market, and the characteristics of those who left and their labour market experiences prior to withdrawing. In the second part of the chapter I ask if the unemployed and those who withdrew from the labour market were less committed to work in the first place; whether their experiences led to a weakening of their commitment to paid work; or whether they remained as committed to paid employment as those in the full-time labour market.

Compared to the numbers of young people who experienced unemployment, the numbers withdrew from the labour market were relatively small. In autumn 1987, when the average age of the cohort was just over 19, around 9 per cent of the year group had withdrawn from the labour market.[1] Females were more than twice as likely as males to have withdrawn (12 per cent as compared to 5 per cent). Young people withdrew from the labour market for a variety of reasons. Some had returned to full-time education while others were working in the home, often with children of their own to look after. Of those who had withdrawn from the labour market, 40 per cent had returned to education, 28 per cent were working in the home and 32 per cent were doing other things.[2] Those who had withdrawn from the labour market

Growing up in a classless society?

TABLE 6.1 Rates of labour market withdrawal six months after respondents reported themselves as being in jobs, unemployed or on schemes (%)

| | Spring 1985 | | | Autumn 1985 | | | Spring 1986 | |
	Male	Female	All	Male	Female	All	Male	Female
Jobs	1	1	1	2	6	4	1	3
Unweighted n (base)	(198)	(183)	(381)	(306)	(275)	(581)	(614)	(557) (11
Unemployed	0	5	2	9	13	11	6	10
Unweighted n (base)	(115)	(89)	(204)	(170)	(133)	(303)	(243)	(201) (4
Scheme – YTS	1	2	1	4	7	5	1	4
Unweighted n (base)	(300)	(222)	(522)	(384)	(299)	(683)	(280)	(274) (5
Scheme – non-YTS								

in order to return to education had similar characteristics to those who had continued their education without entering the labour market, although on average they had slightly fewer O grades. The young women who withdrew from the labour market in order to work in the home had similar social and educational character-istics to the unemployed, the main difference being that they were more likely to be married or cohabiting and have children of their own. Those who had withdrawn for other non-specified reasons also had similar characteristics to the unemployed.

One common factor among those who had withdrawn from the labour market was that they tended to have had substantial experience of unemployment, although this varied according to the sorts of activities they were engaged in after withdrawal. Those who had returned to education spent a mean total of 30 weeks unemployed since leaving school; those who were work-ing in the home 73 weeks; and those who were doing other things 42 weeks. Males tended to have spent more time unemployed than females, although over two-thirds (68 per cent) of women who withdrew from the labour market in order to work in the home had experienced a period of unemployment which was in excess of a year. In all other groups, a smaller proportion had been

Autumn 1986			Spring 1987			Autumn 1987		
Male	Female	All	Male	Female	All	Male	Female	All
2	7	4	1	2	1	2	4	3
(757)	(734)	(1491)	(918)	(987)	(1905)	(959)	(1035)	(1994)
7	16	11	2	9	6	7	16	11
(298)	(234)	(532)	(278)	(251)	(529)	(276)	(233)	(509)
9	6	8	3	10	8	3	16	9
(145)	(145)	(290)	(43)	(43)	(86)	(28)	(26)	(54)
			6	4	3	3	7	4
			(74)	(27)	(101)	(95)	(35)	(130)

unemployed for over a year (see Chapter 5).

Because those who had withdrawn from the labour market tended, on average, to have had a greater experience of unemployment than those in full-time jobs or in full-time education, it is necessary to ask whether there is any relationship between unemployment experience and labour market withdrawal. To answer this question I look first at the proportion of young people who had withdrawn from the labour market after having described themselves as being in full-time jobs, unemployed or on schemes six months earlier (Table 6.1).

In each six-month period, a higher proportion of young people who had been unemployed than those who had been in full-time jobs had withdrawn from the labour market. Females were more likely than males to have withdrawn following a period of unemployment. Westwood (1984) has suggested that domestic life is often seen as attractive by women working in boring or repetitive jobs, although the reality often conflicts with these initial impressions. It would seem likely that young women who are having difficulties finding paid jobs and suffering the effects of prolonged unemployment may also start to regard domestic life as an escape from unemployment.

In the first three time periods, the rate of labour market withdrawal was similar among those on schemes and those in jobs. However, from autumn 1986 onwards (when later labour market entrants and those who had been unemployed or in jobs prior to joining YTS would be finishing their schemes) young people who had previously been on schemes were more likely to have withdrawn from the labour market six months later than those in full-time jobs.

I suggest that many of these unemployed young people had become trapped in a cycle of unemployment and unemployment-based schemes and were finding it increasingly difficult to escape. In such circumstances some young people give up hope of finding work and withdraw from the labour mark_'; this was a course of action which females were more likely to .,ave taken than males. Labour market withdrawal will enable young people to regard themselves as having some control over their life events and to regain some self-esteem as they escape from the cycle of job-search and rejection, with the inevitable sense of failure which accompanies it.

6.2 Work ethics and labour market participation

The work ethics of young people tend to be an emotive subject as those without jobs and those who withdraw from the labour market are often suspected as being 'workshy'. The introduction of youth training schemes at a time when levels of youth unemployment were rising was partly influenced by a concern that young people who spent a part of their formative years without work would not develop a commitment to work. Indeed there is a widespread assumption that: 'young people who remain unemployed for a long time tend to turn away from values and standards that are considered important in our society, as a result of which they are no longer found suitable to take part in the process of labour – not even when there are plenty of jobs' (Jehoel-Gijsbers and Groot, 1989, p. 492). In a recent article in the *Sunday Times*, an American social scientist argued that prolonged contact with unemployment had far-reaching consequences for young men in Britain:

> By remaining out of the workforce during the crucial formative years, young men aren't just losing a few years of job experience. They are missing out on the time in which they need to have been acquiring the skills and the networks of friends and experiences that enable them to establish a place

for themselves – not only in the workplace, but a vantage point from which they can make sense of themselves and their lives (Murray, 1989).

In other words, there is a fear that those experiencing unemployment after leaving school would become a 'lost generation' and would form an underclass of long-term unemployed adults.

I would suggest that such fears are unfounded because by the time they leave school, young people have spent much of their pre-adult lives in preparation for future work roles. They already regard paid employment as forming a central part of their adult lives and are aware that their future incomes and life-styles are dependent upon the sorts of jobs they enter. Indeed, it has been argued that young people without work fantasise about being able to adopt 'normal' life-styles centred around paid employment (Walsgrove, 1987).

It has also been argued that school-leavers have developed a commitment to different aspects of their work. Those who enter, or expect to enter, higher level occupations often see work as central to their overall self-concept and regard it as an important feature of their lives. Through their work achievements they gain much satisfaction. On the other hand, those who enter less skilled jobs tend to see work more as a means to an end (Lodahl and Kejner, 1965; Ashton and Field, 1976). For these people, work is a more peripheral part of their overall self-image from which they expect few inherent satisfactions.

> Many jobs are alienating and produce few rewards. In these circumstances satisfactions are not gained through work but through material rewards or participation in shop floor cultures or collective action. Commitment at this level is not necessarily linked to any of the inherent satisfactions which may be gained from work as an activity. Commitment to work may be simply due to the importance of the material rewards to be gained from employment, in which case lack of satisfaction from life without a job can often be tied to the importance of money. (Furlong, 1988b, p. 122)

This distinction between forms of commitment is important; Ashton (1986) has suggested that employment commitment is often defined in ways which are more appropriate to middle-class attitudes. The middle-class work ethic shares the central assumption of Weber's definition of the Protestant work ethic: work is regarded as a moral duty and people are seen as gaining self-fulfilment through their participation in work. In reality, work holds little intrinsic meaning for a large proportion of the workforce.

In much of the established work on the transition from school to work it was argued, incorrectly, that many of those from the lower working classes and those destined for semi- and unskilled jobs left school with a peripheral interest in work as an area of achievement (Ashton and Field, 1976; Willis, 1977). Recent research has failed to confirm the existence of this 'self-damnation' process. Social class of origin is not directly associated with the centrality of work within young people's overall frame of reference. Work-centred attitudes are regarded as important by many young people from lower working-class homes and by many of those who enter low skill jobs (Furlong, 1988a).

In a longitudinal study of young people in Leicester (Furlong, 1988a), it was discovered that those from lower working-class families saw it as just as important as those from professional and managerial family backgrounds to obtain interesting work and work which they could take a pride in. In other words, the development of work attitudes in young people before leaving school cannot be explained simply in terms of the dynamics of class position as is sometimes implied (Fox, 1971; Willis, 1977). In so far as the family is central to the development of occupational aspirations (Hayes, 1970), social class has a strong influence on developing work attitudes. But other factors, such as school experiences and achievements, gender, and the opportunities available in the local labour market must also be taken into account, as well as an understanding of the ways in which work attitudes are a product of a particular community and work environment (Goldthorpe *et al.*, 1968 and 1969). The combination of these factors produces a set of experiences and these experiences ultimately crystallise into a work attitude.

Young people often place a high value on meaningful work while adopting instrumental attitudes towards the sorts of work they are currently engaged in. Instrumentalism is not a class-based commitment to work (Salaman, 1981) but is best regarded as a *reaction* to work and to expected features of the work environment. Most young people would like to have jobs they could take an interest in and could find rewarding in a non-financial sense. However, in anticipating the work forms they will engage in and using knowledge about work gained in the home and the school, instrumentalism develops as a justification of the value of that work. In other words, it is young people's experiences which are central to the development of work orientations and attitudes.

While recognising that people are committed to different aspects of their work and that those with experience of unsatisfactory work may be committed to their work simply as a means to provide the financial resources necessary to meet their material needs, I now consider the extent to which work attitudes are affected by labour market experiences. In particular, I am interested in whether those who were unemployed or had withdrawn from the labour market had different values and attitudes in relation to work compared with those in jobs or education.

To answer this question I look at the effects of unemployment on young people's employment-commitment and job-search attitudes. The questions relating to employment-commitment and job-search attitudes were each included in one version of the 1986 and 1987 questionnaires and are presented here in the form of scales. The employment-commitment scale was constructed from four statements with which young people were asked to agree or disagree: 'Having almost any job is better than being unemployed'; 'I could easily get enough satisfaction out of life without a job'; 'If you haven't got a job, life is rather pointless and a waste of time'; and 'A person must have a job to feel a full member of society'. Responses to these statements were scored from one to five to indicate the strength of agreement or disagreement with a statement. A score of five was given to those who 'strongly agreed' with a positive statement or 'strongly disagreed' with a negative statement, while a score of one was given to those who 'strongly disagreed' with a positive statement or 'strongly agreed' with a negative statement. The job-search attitude scale was constructed in a similar manner from the responses to three statements: 'I can't be bothered looking for a job any more'; 'I'm looking for a job as hard as I've ever done; and 'It's not worth chasing after jobs nowadays'.

Detailed analysis of young people's responses to these statements demonstrates a high commitment to employment among young people, and those without jobs tend to have positive attitudes in relation to the search for work (Furlong, 1988b). In the 1986 follow-up of the Scottish cohort, a majority of young people agreed that having any job is preferable to being unemployed (63 per cent) and that they would be unable to lead a satisfying life without a job (56 per cent). However, many respondents did not

TABLE 6.2 The effect of unemployment and length of unemployment on job search attitudes and employment commitment

	Job Search Attitude		Employment Commitment	
		Unweighted n		Unweighted n
Status in Autumn 1987				
Full-time education	12.3	(455)	12.5	(459)
Full-time job	12.5	(1012)	12.7	(1020)
Unemployed	11.9	(294)	12.5	(294)
Withdrawn from labour market (reason other than education)	11.9	(91)	13.0	(92)
ANOVA	p=0.0000		p=0.022 ns	
Length of unemployment*				
1– 6 months	12.9	(329)	12.5	(330)
6 months – 1 year	12.5	(147)	12.5	(147)
1 year or more	11.7	(309)	12.5	(312)
ANOVA	p=0.010		p=0.997 ns	

Note: 1. *Length of unemployment since school among those who were unemployed in autumn 1987.

regard it as necessary to have a job in order to be regarded as a full member of society (42 per cent) and a majority did not agree that life would be rather pointless and a waste of time without a job (68 per cent) (Furlong, 1988b).

Most young people without jobs had positive attitudes towards the search for work. In 1986, a majority (85 per cent) did not agree that they 'couldn't be bothered looking for a job any more' and that 'it's not worth chasing after jobs nowadays' (76 per cent). Over two thirds (70 per cent) said that they were 'looking for a job as hard as I've ever done'. Job-search attitude scores varied with young people's current status; those who were unemployed and those who had withdrawn from the labour market for reasons other than education tended to have less positive job-search attitudes than those in full-time jobs or in education (Table 6.2). This variation was similar for males and females. However, there was no significant variation in the employment-commitment of young people whether they were in jobs, unemployed, in education had withdrawn from the labour market for reasons other than education (Furlong, 1988b). Banks and Ullah (1988) have demonstrated a similar relationship between young people's' labour market status and their job-search attitudes and employment-commitment.

Not only was the experience of unemployment associated with more negative job-search attitudes, but total length of unemployment since school also had a significant, but small, detrimental effect (Table 6.2, bottom panel) (see also Banks and Ullah, 1988). Among those who were unemployed in autumn 1987, those who had been unemployed for less than six months had a score of 12·9 while those with a total unemployment of over a year had a score of 11·7.

Prolonged periods of unemployment have this depressing effect on job-search attitudes because young people who are continually rejected in their search for work eventually become discouraged and slightly reduce their job-search efforts (Banks and Ullah, 1988). Thus disillusionment and feeling that it is futile to continue a job-search with the same intensity as at first, coupled with a fear of continued rejection, eventually leads young people to put less effort into finding jobs. Among the Scottish cohort, young people who had not had a job or been on YTS since leaving school tended to have made fewer job applications over the previous three months than those who had had experience of work (Furlong, 1988b).

Reducing the effort put into the search for work can have positive consequences for the unemployed. In a study of unemployed men in the United States, Yancey (1980) discovered that the subjects of his study were protecting their self-confidence by restricting their job-search. Rather than applying for advertised vacancies, these men were concentrating on making casual calls on firms to see if they had any vacancies. Yancey explains that it is regarded as less damaging to one's self confidence to be told that no jobs are available than to be rejected for an advertised vacancy.

To measure the effect of unemployment on employment-commitment, I first measured the mean employment-commitment score in spring 1986 of those in jobs (13·2). I then measured the employment-commitment scores in autumn 1987 for these same people, distinguishing between those who were in full-time jobs in 1987 and those who were unemployed. There was a significant deterioration in employment-commitment for those who were unemployed in 1987 (11·8) while there was a small deterioration for those in jobs (12·7). From this evidence I suggest that unemployment can

Growing up in a classless society?

TABLE 6.3 A comparison of mean work attitude and employment commitment scale values of young people in jobs and unemployed in 1986 who subsequently withdrew from the labour market for reasons other than education, with the mean scores of all those in jobs and unemployed in 1986

	Employment Commitment		Work Attitude	
		Unweighted n		Unweighted n
All in jobs in 1986	13.2	(714)	17.1	(757)
Job in 1986, withdrew over following 18 months	12.9	(23)	17.0	(20)
ANOVA	$p = 0.580$ ns		$p = 0.951$ ns	
All unemployed in 1986	12.5	(255)	14.6	(272)
Unemployed in 1986, withdrew over following 18 months	12.2	(26)	14.1	(17)
ANOVA	$p = 0.459$ ns		$p = 0.478$ ns	

have a detrimental affect on employment-commitment. However, when I examined employment-commitment among those who were unemployed in autumn 1987 in relation to their total unemployment since school, I found no variation whatsoever. This suggests that becoming unemployed after having had a job can result in a deterioration in employment-commitment, but that once unemployed a person's commitment to employment does not continue to decline.

Finally, I wished to test whether there was a relationship between young people's attitudes towards work and subsequent labour market withdrawal. To examine this question, I used the employment-commitment scale again and also used a new scale to represent 'work-attitudes'. The questions which were used to form the work-attitude scale appear only in the 1986 questionnaire and were in a different version to that which contained the employment-commitment questions. The scale was constructed in the same way as the employment-commitment scale using six questions: 'Most of the jobs available to people like me are pretty awful'; 'The staff at the Careers Office do their best for people like me'; 'Most employers look upon people like me as a form of cheap labour'; 'Most people like me have little chance of finding a job'; 'The staff at the Careers Office don't really care whether people like me get a job'; 'Most of the jobs available to people like me are worth having'.

First, I compared the employment-commitment and work-attitudes of young people in jobs in 1986 who left the labour market for reasons other than education between spring 1986 and autumn 1987 with the mean scores of all those in jobs in 1986. Those who withdrew had slightly lower mean employment-commitment and work-attitude scores, but neither were statistically significant (Table 6.3).

Second, I compared the employment-commitment and work-attitudes of young people who said they were 'unemployed and looking for work' in 1986 but who left the labour market for reasons other than education between spring 1986 and autumn 1987, with the mean scores of all of those who were unemployed in spring 1986. In terms of both employment-commitment and work-attitude scores, there was no statistically significant difference between the two groups.

In sum, the evidence presented here suggests that unemployment and length of unemployment does not result in a deterioration in employment-commitment, although in cases where young people had previously had a job, losing the job can be accompanied by a lowering of employment-commitment. In contrast, young people who become unemployed do become discouraged in their search for work and this may have an effect on their job-search attitudes. Unemployment was associated with a slightly more negative job-search attitude, and length of unemployment was associated with declining job-search attitudes scores.

The picture among young people who had withdrawn from the labour market was rather different. Those who had jobs before withdrawing from the labour market had similar levels of employment-commitment and similar work-attitudes to those who remained in jobs. And among those who were unemployed prior to withdrawing, I found that their employment-commitment and work-attitudes were similar to those who remained unemployed. In other words, there is no evidence to suggest that young people who withdraw from the labour market do so because they have a lower initial commitment to work or have less favourable work attitudes. Nor is it true that their commitment becomes reduced due to prolonged experience of unemployment.

These conclusions are supported by a longitudinal study of young people in Holland (Jehoel-Gijsbers and Groot, 1989) which included similar work-attitude scales. Jehoel-Gijsbers and Groot began with the hypothesis that young people without jobs were likely to adapt to their situation by attaching less value to work. Because young people are at a critical phase in their development, a period of unemployment soon after leaving school may give them less opportunity to learn positive value-orientations towards work. However, through their research they also discovered that value-orientations did not change much with duration of unemployment or position in the labour market, and they concluded that orientations were developed during primary and secondary socialisation and were relatively unaffected by labour market experience.

6.3 Conclusion

There are many myths and half-truths which surround the issues of young people's work attitudes and their withdrawal from the labour market. In terms of qualifications, young people who withdraw from the labour market but who do not return to education are barely distinguishable from the unemployed and those working in semi- and unskilled jobs. However, an examination of labour market histories leads to the conclusion that withdrawal is most common among those with prolonged experience of unemployment.

I have suggested that once a young person gives up hope of finding work, withdrawal becomes an option which can bring positive psychological benefits. For young women, especially those who are married or have children, labour market withdrawal is often a socially acceptable alternative to unemployment.

One of the fears commonly expressed about youth unemployment is that school-leavers who do not find jobs will fail to develop positive work attitudes and ethics. The lack of such ethics would further disadvantage them in the labour market and they would be in danger of becoming a 'lost generation' or an underclass. I have argued that these fears are unfounded largely because young people develop a commitment to work long before they leave school. Some will have developed a commitment to work as a means of gaining self-fulfilment, while others are committed becasuse of a realisation that work holds the key to their material satisfactions and to their enjoyment of non-work time.

Those who were working tended to have higher levels of work commitment than those who were unemployed or who had withdrawn from the labour market, but I argue that these differences arise through young people's labour market experiences. Because work-commitment is reduced as a result of unemployment, it cannot be said to be a cause of unemployment or labour market withdrawal.

Notes

1. Withdrawers were defined as young people who had reported themselves as in jobs, on schemes or unemployed at some stage, yet subsequently described themselves as being in full-time education, working full-time in the the home, or 'doing something else.'
2. Some of those who had withdrawn from the labour market described themselves as 'doing something else'. We have little information on these young people; some will have been unemployed but not seeking work (perhaps waiting to enter a specific job or course), while others may simply have had a reservation about ticking one of the main status category boxes on the questionnaire.

7

THE DEVELOPMENT OF OCCUPTIONAL ASPIRATIONS

7.1 Introduction

Before they leave school, young people have often developed strong impressions about the sorts of experiences which are in store for them beyond the school gates. During childhood and adolescence, through their experiences in the home and school, young people gradually build up impressions of their future roles and positions in society. These impressions are important to an understanding of recruitment because they have a bearing on young people's expectations and the sorts of jobs they seek within the labour market (Hayes, 1970).

Before I go on to discuss the process of occupational recruitment in Chapter 8, in this chapter I examine the development of occupational aspirations in young people. This analysis confirms earlier research which has shown that occupational aspirations reflect the deeply-embedded impressions about the world which have developed as a result of experiences in the family and in the school. Furthermore, I suggest that aspirations are important to an understanding of the transition from school to work and that recent changes in the labour market and new training arrangements, while unlikely to have raised young people's aspirations, have led to a situation in which young people frequently have to make downward modifications to their aspirations.

7.2 Occupational Socialisation

Young people's knowledge of work originates largely from parents and other family members; and the sorts of work experienced by members of a family tend to be significant in shaping the occupational horizons of younger family members (Paul, 1962; Hayes, 1970). In studies where young people have been asked about the sources of their labour market knowledge, they have tended to name members of their own family or other close personal contacts (Carter, 1962; Hayes, 1970; Furlong, 1988a). Yet family experiences tend to be confined to a fairly narrow sector of the local labour market and this can result in narrow occupational horizons among young people.

During childhood young people internalise many of the taken-for-granted assumptions held by family members and these assumptions have an effect on the ways in which they are orientated towards the labour market. As a result of differential patterns of socialisation, it has been suggested that young people from lower working-class families tend to come to seek their pleasures in the immediate present, while those from middle-class and upper working-class families learn to postpone gratification (Ashton and Field, 1976). These differences in frames of reference have implications for young people's entry into the labour market, as skilled and high-status jobs tend to be characterised by a career structure in which initial rewards are relatively poor, but which offer relatively good prospects in the long term. In contrast, those who enter unskilled jobs are often paid relatively high wages on entry, although such jobs offer few prospects for future advancement.

Because of the role of the family in imparting occupational knowledge it has often been suggested that young people tend to enter the labour market with occupational aspirations which confirm their class backgrounds. Willis (1977), for example, has suggested that boys from lower working-class families tend to be culturally orientated towards manual labour, through which they can demonstrate their rejection of middle-class values and prove their masculinity to their friends and families. Yet Willis's position can be rather misleading unless it is put into perspective: many researchers have noted that young people from lower working-class families frequently aspire towards higher positions within the labour market than those in which they are eventually placed. The small group of young males on whom Willis based his study did not hold attitudes which were typical among working-class youths. Brown (1987b), for example, has shown that it is much more common to find working-class pupils who are willing to make some effort at school in order to secure entry into 'respectable' working-class jobs.

There is a strong body of research which has shown that young people from lower working-class families often enter the labour market hoping for 'something more' than a semi- or un-skilled job (Douvan and Adelson, 1966; Brown, 1987b; Furlong,

1988a). Initial aspirations may be 'cooled-out' as a result of experiences in the labour market, and certain behaviours in the labour market (such as job changing and reluctance to accept 'dead-end' jobs) can often be explained in terms of attempts to fulfil early aspirations.

While the home is central to an understanding of the development of occupational aspirations, family influence is mediated by other agencies such as the school and the peer group. The school affects occupational choices through a process of anticipatory socialisation (Musgrave, 1967): teacher expectations not only affect their pupils' school performance, but can influence occupational horizons. High achievers are encouraged to consider further or higher education, while low achievers may be encouraged to leave school at the minimum age. Although 'bright' working-class children may broaden their occupational horizons as a result of encouragement at school, teacher expectations often serve as a mechanism through which young people's initial impressions of their future place within the labour market are confirmed. In a study of two schools in Leicestershire, teachers were asked to complete occupational assessment forms on their pupils (Furlong, 1988a). These assessments tended to be strongly related to the pupils' social class. As a result of the tendency for young people from working-class families to underachieve at school, occupational assessments made by teachers often reflect class inequalities. Social class influences academic achievement and, in turn, academic achievement influences young people's aspirations and expectations (Marini and Greenberger, 1978).

The ways in which education is organised can also be important in helping young people to broaden their occupational horizons and break away from class-congruent roles. Roberts (1973) has shown, for example, how the 'climate of expectation' of one's future prospects tends to vary according to the type of educational institution attended (also West and Newton, 1983). Indeed, the recognition that schools have the potential to provide a framework within which young people's occupational self-concepts are capable of development has led to changes in the organisation of education. In Britain this was one of the factors behind the abolition of the 'tripartite' system (Ford, 1969). Although the introduction of Comprehensive schools has promoted a greater social mix within schools than was the case previously, supporters of the tripartite system have argued that young people from working-class homes who attend Grammar schools are likely to develop broader occupational horizons as a result of the climate of expectation within these schools.

While the school ethos and teacher expectations are important, a working-class child in a primarily working-class school is much more likely to mix exclusively with working-class friends than is the same child within a primarily middle-class school (Turner, 1964). In turn, the social composition of the peer group will have an effect upon the aspirations of its members as a consensus emerges as to an 'acceptable' range of occupations (Furlong, 1988a). As young people's occupational self-concepts develop and are incorporated into their overall self-image, so they tend to mix with friends who share a similar future. Turner (1964) discovered that peer groups tend to develop more along lines of occupational aspirations than along strictly class background lines. This is supported by evidence from the Leicester study where it was found that few young people had friends with occupational aspirations far above or below their own (Furlong, 1988a).

Indeed, those with aspirations outside their class of origin often face derision at school if they mix with friends of a similar background who lack such aspirations (Bain and Anderson, 1974). As a result, they must either learn to put up with the derision, or else mix with people holding similar aspirations. Thus people tend to adopt the attitudes and values of the groups they belong to and anticipate their future class membership by learning in advance the 'appropriate' attitudes (Turner, 1964). Young people from the working classes who aspire to middle-class positions come to regard themselves as members of the middle-class and adopt values befitting a member of that class, through membership of a predominantly middle-class peer group.

Careers programmes within schools were partly developed in order to prevent the premature closure of occupational horizons, so in this context it is important to assess the influence of careers education on young people's occupational aspirations. As the scarcity of jobs for young people began to concern educationalists, many schools developed and extended their careers programmes and teachers took positive steps to ensure that their pupils The theoretical justification for contemporary careers education programmes and the position of the Careers Officer within the programme stemmed largely from the work of Ginzberg and colleagues (1951) and Super (1968). In this model, occupational 'choice' is presented as a developmental process in which individuals 'seek the optimal fit between their career preparation and goals and the realities of the world of work'. Thus, occupational 'choice' is seen as the process of developing and implementing a self concept. Individuals are seen as choosing an occupation on the basis of the congruence of a particular occupation with their self-concept. The purpose of the careers programme is to help young people achieve vocational maturity, and 'to extend the range of their thinking about opportunities in work and in life generally' (Department of Education and Science, 1973, p. 6).

As levels of youth unemployment rose during the 1980s, the Ginzberg-Super model became unfashionable and was criticised for presenting the process as being a very conscious affair. Roberts (1968), for example, rejected the notion that entry into an occupation could be understood in terms of the implementation of a self-concept for less able and socially disadvantaged young people. He suggested substituting the concept of 'opportunity structure' to provide a more adequate understanding of occupational entry. For Roberts, ambitions are to a large extent based upon the occupation a person expects to enter rather than one a person would ideally like to enter. In other words, ambitions are seen as a subjective interpretation of objective reality.

Although Ginzberg and Super regard the individual as the 'prime-mover' in the process, occupational 'choice' is ultimately seen as a compromise between a person's interests, capacities and values and 'reality factors' such as the available opportunities which act as parameters. Neither Ginzberg nor Super neglected the structural constraints on action, as Roberts has suggested. Ginzberg and Super argued that individuals build up an occupational self-concept through their experiences in the 'real world', and therefore the occupational self-concept is shaped by the constraints of that world.

A careers programme influenced by the Ginzberg-Super model tends to be run in a non-directive manner. Teachers, rather than suggesting jobs to young people, prefer them to reach their own conclusions about their suitability for particular types of work. In contrast, those adopting a structural philosophy tend to take a more directive stance and help individuals adjust to the opportunity structures to which they have access. Counsellors adopting this approach would be more prone to make suggestions to young people.

Either way, when success is judged by the consumers, poor levels of satisfaction with the Careers Service are commonly reported (Jahoda and Chalmers, 1963; Maizels, 1970; West and Newton, 1983). Those who devise careers education programmes face a daunting task in challenging the restricting influences of the family and school on the range of occupations towards which young people are orientated. Careers programmes are unlikely to be able to exert a major influence on occupational horizons unless they can operate at a level at which they can start to challenge the taken-for-granted assumptions held by young people about their future lives. Yet despite its handicaps, there is evidence that developmental careers work has had some success in expanding young people's occupational horizons and in encouraging them to raise their sights (West and Newton, 1983). Indeed, developmental careers work has even been criticised for its effectiveness in raising aspirations (Roberts, 1975). This is because the broadening of occupational horizons may only cause young people distress if they must make downward modifications in their aspirations in the light of opportunities available locally (West and Newton, 1983).

While young people in Britain are often portrayed as leaving school with fairly realistic aspirations (Ashton and Field, 1976), it is frequently suggested that in America young people often leave school with unrealistically high aspirations which are subsequently 'cooled-out' within the labour market (Millar and Form, 1951; Douvan and Adelson, 1966; Kerckoff, 1990). These differences in occupational aspirations tend to be explained as being a consequence of the differences between the British and American education systems. The North American educational system has a lower degree of stratification than the English or Scottish systems.[1] The early closure of occupational horizons is largely prevented in North America through the system's close approximation to Turner's (1961) 'contest mobility' model. Hence, young people's occupational horizons tend to remain fairly broad until quite late into school life. In Britain it has been suggested that young people's experiences within the educational system leave them with fewer illusions and they often have relatively narrow occupational horizons at a young age (Ashton and Field, 1976).

Evidence from the 1989 Scottish cohort[2] challenges two of the assumptions made in earlier literature: that young people in Scotland leave school with narrow aspirations because stratification within the education system leaves them with few illusions about

TABLE 7.1 'What job do you hope to be doing in five or six years' time?', by social class and fourth year SCE attainment (%)

	Professional and Managerial Careers	Skilled Manual and Clerical Careers	Semi & Unskilled Service & Manual Jobs	Don't know Unclassifiable	Out of the Labour Market	Total	Unweighted n
Professional and Managerial Class							
Male	52	16	12	17	3	100	(74)
Female	51	22	5	18	3	99	(82)
All	51	19	8	18	3	99	(157)
Upper Working Class							
Male	28	34	22	14	3	101	(83)
Female	34	36	9	18	3	100	(92)
All	31	35	15	16	3	100	(176)
Lower Working Class							
Male	23	29	30	17	1	100	(35)
Female	30	39	10	19	2	100	(36)
All	26	34	20	18	1	99	(71)
5 or more O Grades							
Male	59	12	6	18	5	100	(95)
Female	59	16	2	20	3	100	(114)
All	59	15	3	19	4	100	(210)
1 – 4 0 Grades							
Male	24	38	22	14	1	99	(81)
Female	28	41	11	17	3	100	(96)
All	26	39	16	16	2	99	(177)
No O Grade Passes							
Male	18	32	31	16	3	100	(55)
Female	19	40	18	20	3	100	(47)
All	18	26	25	18	3	100	(102)

their future position in the labour market; and that young people from lower working-class families seek unskilled work as part of a rejection of the middle-class values of the school and as a celebration of working-class culture.

In the first questionnaire sent to members of 1989 Scottish cohort, young people were asked, 'What job do you hope to be doing in five or six years time?'. Responses to this open-ended question were grouped into three occupational categories: professional and related and managerial careers; skilled manual and clerical careers; and semi- and unskilled manual and service jobs.[3] Over a third of respondents said that they hoped to be working in a professional and related or managerial career (35 per cent); just over a quarter hoped to be working in skilled manual or clerical occupations (26 per cent); while just over one in ten hoped to be working in semi- and unskilled service and manual jobs (13 per cent) The occupations to which members of the cohort aspired varied by social class, but within each class a small minority of young people hoped to enter semi- and unskilled jobs. Willis's work is put into perspective by the Scottish sample in which just one in five young people from the lower working-class (20 per cent) hoped to enter this category of work, compared to 15 per cent of those from upper working-class families and 8 per cent of those from the middle-classes. In fact just over a quarter of those from the lower working-class hoped to enter professional and related and managerial careers (26 per cent), compared to almost a third of those from the upper working-class (31 per cent) and just over half of those from the middle classes (Table 7.1).

Among members of each social class, school attainments can be expected to affect occupational aspirations as young people come to adjust their assumptions in the light of the signals received at school (Hopson and Hayes, 1972; Ryrie *et al.*, 1983; Kelly, 1989). Occupational aspirations among the Scottish sample were strongly correlated with the total qualifications they had gained by the end of fourth year. A majority of young people with five or more O grade passes hoped to be working in professional and related and managerial careers (59 per cent), as compared to just over a quarter of those with between one and four O grades (26 per cent) and fewer than one in five of those with no O grade passes (18 per cent) (Table 7.1). While very few qualified young people hoped to be working in semi- and unskilled jobs, even among the unqualified only a quarter (25 per cent) hoped to be working in these occupations. Recent longitudinal work on the development of career preferences among school children (Kelly, 1989) has demonstrated the existence of a relationship between academic performance and career aspirations at the ages of 11, 14 and 17. Furthermore, Kelly has shown that for boys the relationship between aspirations and academic performance becomes stronger between the ages of 11 and 17, while academically able girls appeared to make downward adjustments in their aspirations and started to select white-collar jobs rather than professional and managerial jobs. These findings are important because, while the strength of class and academic performance on the development of occupational aspirations has been discussed extensively in the literature, there is still a tendency to assume that the process operates in a similar manner for both sexes. Kelly's evidence and that presented in Table 7.1 show that these assumptions are wrong.

Among the Scottish sample, within each social class and within each attainment band, young women tended to hope for a higher level of occupation than young men. In particular, very few young women in any group hoped to be working in semi- and unskilled service and manual jobs. Among young women from the lower working-class, for example, only one in ten expressed a desire to enter such occupations (10 per cent), including fewer than one in five (18 per cent) of those with no O grade passes. In contrast, nearly a third of males from the lower working-class (30 per cent) and with no O grade passes (31 per cent) hoped to be working in semi- and unskilled service and manual jobs.

Although females leave school with higher occupational aspirations than males, their aspirations tend to be confined to a much narrower range of occupations such as office jobs, skilled service jobs, and work in the 'caring' professions. Many researchers have tried to explain this by reference to the differential experiences of boys and girls in the school (e.g. Delamont, 1980). Although teachers may expect girls to behave in certain ways and may regard particular subjects and activities as being inappropriate, the position of girls within the educational system has shown marked improvement over the past decade (Chapter 2). In a study of young people in Leicester, girls were often seen by their teachers as more academically competent than boys and were judged as being more likely than boys to enter a professional occupation (Furlong, 1986).

Despite any trend towards equalisation within the school, girls and boys still tend to experience distinct patterns of socialisation within the home and encounter different expectations within their peer groups. Of particular relevance to the development of occupational aspirations is the argument that the socialisation of girls tends to produce a gender identity which is focused upon future marital roles. Although marriage and motherhood no longer signal the end of a woman's career (Hakim, 1979; Martin and Roberts, 1984), it is often suggested that girls tend to see their future roles as wives and mothers as being more important than their roles in the labour market (Douvan and Adelson, 1966). Recent studies have demonstrated, however, that most young women show little preoccupation with marriage. The adolescents in Griffin's (1985) study, for example, saw marriage and mother-hood as 'distant if inevitable events'. The proportion of young women among the Scottish cohort who said that they hoped to be out of the labour market in five or six years' time was similar to the proportion of young men (around 3 per cent).

Differences in the occupational aspirations of males and females strongly reflect the sexual segregation of the labour market. Indeed, the sexual segregation of the labour market imposes a serious constraint on occupational aspirations and helps to exclude young women from many of the high-pay and high-status career paths. Sharpe has argued that the structure of occu-pational opportunities commonly available to women in a given generation shapes the aspirations of the next generation: 'Every generation of girls grows up within a family situation which is trying to adapt and survive within present economic and social conditions, and eventually plays its own part in continuing this process' (Sharpe, 1976, p. 46). Girls tend to leave school with occupational aspirations which are focused towards the narrow range of jobs women hold in the wider society. In a comprehen-sive study of fifth form girls in England, Rauta and Hunt con-cluded that the range of jobs that the girls aspired to were 'largely confined to those which were either mainly carried out by women or have opened their doors least reluctantly to women' (Rauta and Hunt, 1972, p. 49). From an early age, girls tend to aspire towards typically 'female' occupations while males aspire to-wards typically 'male' occupations. Even at age 11, Kelly found that only two jobs (Police Officer and Vet) appeared in the 'top ten' of jobs for which both boys and girls aspired (Kelly, 1989).

TABLE 7.2 'What job do you hope to be doing in five or six years' time?', by current status and experience of the Youth Training Scheme (%)

	Professional and Managerial Careers	Skilled Manual and Clerical Careers	Semi & Unskilled Service & Manual Jobs	Don't know Unclassifiable	Out of the Labour Market	Total	Unweighted n
Currently in Education							
Male	49	21	7	19	4	100	(130)
Female	47	28	4	18	2	99	(174)
All	48	25	6	19	3	101	(305)
Currently in Labour Market							
Male	17	35	32	13	2	99	(103)
Female	23	35	17	19	4	98	(85)
All	20	36	26	16	3	101	(189)
Experience of YTS							
Male	15	38	34	12	2	101	(65)
Female	19	40	19	17	4	99	(54)
All	17	39	27	14	3	100	(119)

Furthermore, there tends to be a close relationship between the degree of sex segregation in occupational aspirations before labour market entry and the degree of sex segregation within the labour market (Marini and Greenberger, 1978).

Among the Scottish sample, differences in level of aspiration between males and females partly reflected the greater tendency of young women to participate in post-compulsory education. Those who were in full-time education at the time of the survey (55 per cent of the cohort) tended to have higher aspirations than those who had entered the labour market (45 per cent of the cohort) (Table 7.2). Those participating in post-compulsory education also tended to be those with the highest levels of educational attainment and those from advantaged social backgrounds. The differences in aspiration at this stage also reflect a 'cooling-out' process which occurs among labour market entrants. While young people in education can hold on to 'unrealistically' high aspirations, those who enter the labour market have to come to terms with reality to a greater extent.

The aspirations of members of the Scottish cohort casts doubt on the general applicability of Turner's model; minimum-age school-leavers in Scotland do not enter the labour market with aspirations focused on the narrow range of occupational positions that they will occupy within the labour market. Around one in five young people who had entered the labour market hoped to enter professional and related and managerial occupations within five or six years. Only just over a quarter (26 per cent) of those in the labour market said that they hoped to be working in semi- and unskilled jobs in five or six years. It would appear that experience in the labour market leads young people in Scotland to make downward adjustments in their aspirations in the same way as young people in the United States do, although the process is a slow one as many young people in jobs express hopes of moving to higher skilled jobs. Indeed, while just one per cent of those in jobs in spring 1989 were working in professional and related and managerial positions, 31 per cent of those in jobs said that they hoped to be working in this sort of occupation in five or six years' time. While a third of those in jobs were working in semi- and unskilled occupations (34 per cent), just under one in five (19 per cent) said that they hoped to be working in these occupations in five or six years' time.

Although educational participation was associated with high

occupational aspirations, those who left school to join YTS tended not to be as insulated from the realities of the labour market. The occupational aspirations of trainees were slightly lower than the aspirations of other young people in the labour market – which may reflect the uncertainty faced by many trainees.

Many aspects of young people's social experience have a bearing on the sorts of occupation they aspire to, yet because many of these experiences overlap, it is difficult to pinpoint those which have the greatest effect on occupational aspirations. For example, social class is associated with school attainment, and qualifications affect young people's post-school experiences and their expectations about their future labour market participation. In order to assess the relative influences of different aspects of young people's social background, attainments and experiences on their occupational aspirations further analysis was conducted using multiple regression (Appendix II).

Educational experience and attainments were found to have a powerful effect on occupational aspirations of males and females. Males who were in education at the time of the survey and males with five or more O grades had significantly higher aspirations, as did females with between one and four O grades and five or more O grades. To some extent, variables measuring educational attainment in the regression model act as proxies for the effects of social class. Nevertheless, young people from middle-class families tend to have significantly higher occupational aspirations than young people from the working-classes, irrespective of qualifications.

Young people's current jobs will inevitably affect the sorts of jobs they hope to enter in five or six years' time. Males in clerical or skilled manual jobs and professional and managerial jobs had aspirations which were significantly higher than those in semi- and unskilled jobs, as did females in professional and managerial occupations. Interestingly, experience of YTS was associated with a decline in occupational aspirations for both males and females (significant for females only). This also suggests that young people's aspirations were 'cooled-out' by YTS, although longitudinal evidence is required to confirm this apparent trend.

7.3 Conclusion

The evidence examined in this chapter challenges some of the assumptions held by other writers on the transition from school to work. In particular, I have suggested that experiences within the family, the peer group and the school do not always lead to a situation where occupational aspirations match the opportunities available to young people with certain characteristics within the labour market. Although school-leavers have a reasonable idea about the sorts of opportunities available to them in the labour market, many young people maintain hopes of entering higher-level occupations. Experience in the labour market is likely to lead eventually to a downward modification in their aspirations.

In this context, Roberts (1975) is correct in his argument that occupational entry is more accurately understood in terms of the opportunities available to young people within the labour market rather than as part of a process in which they manage to implement their occupational aspirations. But an understanding of occupational aspirations is important, both because they are not simply a reflection of available opportunities and because they enable us to examine the experience of the transition on a subjective level.

Young people are not the passive products of socialising forces, and their desires are not shaped simply through their personal experiences within the social structure. If our subjective impressions reflected objective reality, then the transition from school to work would be a universally smooth process as our expectations would be fulfilled. Because our hopes are not constrained by reality factors, the transition can be regarded as a difficult period in many young people's lives when they are forced to make downward adjustments in order to come to terms with the local structure of opportunities.

Notes

1. The Scottish education system can be regarded as less stratified than the English system, given the more widespread adoption of Comprehensive schools.
2., The 1989 cohort of the Scottish Young People's Survey is described in Appendix I.
3. Around 8 per cent said that they didn't know what job they hoped to be working in; 3 per cent said that they hoped to be out of the labour market; and 9 per cent of responses could not be classified because the answer given was too vague (such as 'working with animals').

8

ENTERING THE WORLD OF WORK

8.1 Introduction

Young people's entry into the world of work is a highly structured process: the culmination of a series of events in which social class affects educational outcomes which in turn affect the sorts of routes they follow from school to work and the types of jobs they enter. Educational achievements, the likelihood of following certain routes into the labour market and the sorts of jobs young people eventually enter are also affected by the area a young person lives in. The social composition of the area will affect attitudes towards education, performance at school and the probability of entering post-compulsory education. Indeed, there is evidence to suggest that neighbourhood deprivation can affect school-leaving qualifications among otherwise comparable young people by between two and four O grades (Garner, 1989). These additional qualifications can be significant in helping young people to enter higher-level occupations. Furthermore, although routes followed into the labour market reflect educational attainments and lead towards certain sectors of the labour market, following a route which includes YTS participation or a period of unemployment can have a powerful effect on the sorts of jobs young people are likely to enter as well as their chances of being employed at all.

In the previous chapter I considered the extent to which occupational aspirations could be used to explain the process of job entry. In this chapter I focus on the process of job allocation by looking at the occupations entered by members of the Scottish cohort in relation to their characteristics and to features of the local labour market within which they made the transition. Because of the increased protraction of the transition from school to work, it is also important to examine the ways in which different post-school experiences affected the probability of entering certain sorts of jobs.

8. 2 Occupational entry and methods of recruitment

In recent years there has been a lively debate within sociology about the nature of the youth labour market and the extent to which it is separate from the adult labour market. This debate was largely fuelled by concerns over whether the jobs lost to young people during the recession of the early 1980s would reappear once the economy recovered.

On the one hand, it was argued that young people had suffered disproportionately compared with adults during the recession largely because of their position at the back of any hiring queue (Thurow, 1975) – and because, having just entered the labour market, they were seeking jobs at a bad moment (Raffe, 1986b). On the other hand, those who saw the problem in structural terms argued that young people were disadvantaged within the labour market because of the separation between the youth and adult labour markets. Structuralists regard the youth labour market as being comprised mainly of low-skill jobs which are particularly vulnerable during a recession; moreover, they argue that changes in the occupational structure mean that many of the low-skill jobs which make up the youth labour market are unlikely to reappear once the economy recovered (Ashton and Maguire, 1983) and this would have serious repercussions for young people.

The debate over the nature of the youth labour market is still unresolved, although it is clear that employers do not consider it appropriate to recruit young people for certain jobs, nor older workers for other jobs (Ashton *et al.*, 1990). Studies of young people's experiences within the labour market have demonstrated considerably greater levels of flexibility in occupational entry patterns than has been suggested by studies of employers (Furlong, 1990b) and suggest a degree of overlap between youth and adult labour markets.

The structure of the labour market for young people has important implications for young people's transition from school to work, as the age structure of occupational opportunities will have a bearing on their ability to follow particular routes into the labour market. Young people who stay on at school beyond the minimum age may find that certain career opportunities (such as apprenticeships) are no longer available to them as a result of age restrictions on entry. The operation of age restrictions in jobs regarded as desirable by many young people, together with the monopolisation of routes into many trades by YTS, provides an

TABLE 8.1 Occupation in 1987 by post–16 experience (%)

		Managerial, Professional and Related	Clerical & Secretarial	Sales	Personal Service	Craft & Skilled Manual	Operatives & Labourers	Forces	Unclassified	Total	Unweighted n
All	Male	6	10	6	9	30	32	6	1	100	(1051)
	Female	10	38	10	22	1	19	1	*	101	(1117)
	All	8	23	8	15	16	26	3	1	100	(2250)
YTS Experience	Male	5	6	6	8	32	38	4	1	100	(496)
	Female	4	35	13	22	*	24	*	*	98	(416)
	All	4	19	9	14	18	32	2	1	99	(912)
No YTS	Male	7	13	7	8	29	26	9	1	100	(542)
	Female	14	40	7	20	1	15	2	*	99	(688)
	All	11	27	7	14	14	20	5	1	99	(1230)
Fifth Year Experience	Male	12	25	7	8	24	18	6	1	101	(433)
	Female	19	52	7	12	1	7	1	0	99	(571)
	All	6	39	7	10	12	12	4	*	100	(1004)
Sixth Year Experience	Male	12	39	9	8	10	12	10	0	100	(156)
	Female	26	48	7	9	*	8	1	0	99	(224)
	All	20	44	8	9	4	10	5	0	100	(380)
NAFE Experience	Male	12	9	10	13	22	22	8	2	98	(151)
	Female	19	34	10	28	1	8	*	0	100	(289)
	All	16	25	10	22	9	13	3	1	99	(440)

incentive for young people who are capable of gaining advanced qualifications to 'risk' YTS rather than stay in education. To this extent Ashton and colleagues are correct when they argue that 'the existing institutional structures are helping to produce a large pool of relatively unskilled youth labour for which there is a declining demand. At the same time these institutional structures are hindering the creation of a more highly educated labour force for which there is an increasing demand' (Ashton *et al.*, 1990, p. 6).

Among the Scottish cohort, just less than half of those who were employed at the age of 19 were working in relatively low skilled segments of the labour market such as semi- and unskilled manual jobs, sales and personal service jobs. The pattern of occupational distribution strongly reflected patterns of sex segregation evident in the broader labour market. A majority of males (62 per cent) worked in manual occupations, with just under half of these employed in craft and skilled manual positions. Relatively few males worked in sales and personal service occupations (15 per cent) and few worked in managerial, professional and clerical occupations (16 per cent). In contrast, almost half the females (48 per cent) worked in managerial, professional and clerical occupations and nearly a third worked in sales and personal service occupations (32 per cent). Only about one in five females (20 per cent) worked in a manual occupation with only 1 per cent working in craft and skilled manual occupations (Table 8. 1, top panel).

Those who stayed on at school into the fifth or sixth year were more likely than others to be working in managerial, professional and clerical occupations (Table 8. 1, bottom panel). Just over half of the males who started a sixth year (51 per cent) and almost three-quarters of the females (74 per cent), were working in managerial, professional and clerical occupations (as compared with 16 per cent and 48 per cent respectively among the cohort as a whole).[1] Conversely, experience of either fifth or sixth year reduced the likelihood of young people of either sex working as operatives and labourers, or working in personal service or sales occupations. For males, experience of fifth or sixth year also reduced the likelihood of their entering craft or skilled manual occupations, although if the analysis is confined to those who entered fifth year without going on to enter sixth year (many of these would be 'conscripts') we find that these young men were not disadvantaged in this respect (Furlong and Raffe, 1989). Those who experienced Non-Advanced Further Education (NAFE) displayed a similar pattern of occupational distribution to those experiencing post-16 education at school, although a relatively high proportion entered personal service occupations after NAFE. (Many took pre-vocational courses linked to personal service occupations such as hairdressing.)

The occupations entered by young people who had experienced YTS were quite different from the jobs entered by those who entered the labour market without experiencing YTS. Ex-trainees were more likely to work in sales, craft and skilled manual occupations and as operatives and labourers, while those who had not experienced YTS were more likely to work in managerial, professional and related and clerical and secretarial occupations. The pattern was similar for males and females. The concentration of ex-YTS trainees in unskilled manual, sales and personal service occupations (together with their tendency to have fewer school qualifications) increases their vulnerability to unemployment. Those who trained in skilled manual jobs while on YTS were in a relatively advantaged position: fewer than one in four were unemployed or out of the labour market at the age of 19. In contrast, almost half of those who trained in personal service occupations (49 per cent) and more than four in ten of those who trained in sales occupations were unemployed or out of the labour market at this stage (Furlong and Raffe, 1989).

While it has been quite common to explain variations in young people's labour market experiences solely in terms of factors which measure personal attainments such as qualifications, it is clear that the structure of the youth labour market has an independent influence on young people's movement within the labour market. Ashton and Sung (1991) have argued that explanations of transitions within the labour market have to take account of the segmented nature of the labour market. Unemployment, for example, is experienced more frequently by those with few qualifications because they have a greater tendency to enter unstable segments of the labour market.

On one level, the occupational distribution and the unemployment chances of the Scottish cohort can be seen as a reflection of the young people's prior attainments. Those who stayed on at school for fifth or sixth year, for example (with the exception of fifth-year conscripts), tended to be better qualified than those who left school at the minimum age, while YTS trainees tended to have fewer qualifications than those who entered jobs directly. Young

TABLE 8.2 Occupational distribution in autumn 1987 by total
SCEs at the end of fourth year (%)

	No Award/ DE Only			1 – 4 O Grades			5+ O Grades		
	All	Male	Female	All	Male	Fernale	All	Male	Female
Managerial, Professional and Related	2	1	3	6	5	8	19	16	21
Clerical and Secretarial	7	2	13	24	8	42	44	25	60
Sales	10	7	14	8	6	10	5	6	4
Personal Service	21	11	13	14	8	20	8	5	9
Craft and Skilled Manual	14	24	1	19	36	1	14	28	1
Operatives and Labourers	41	45	35	25	32	17	8	12	4
Armed Forces	4	7	0	3	5	1	3	7	2
Unclassified	1	1	1	*	1	0	*	1	0
Total	100	98	100	99	101	99	101	100	101
Unweighted n	(483)	(258)	(225)	(933)	(457)	(476)	(750)	(335)	(415)

Note: * = less than 0.5 per cent.

people who had gained five or more O grades by the end of the
fourth year were more likely than those with fewer O grades to be
working in managerial, professional and clerical occupations in
autumn 1987 (Table 8. 2). In contrast, young people with no O
grade passes were over-represented among operatives and labourers, in personal service occupations and in sales occupations.
Those in the middle qualification band (with between one and
four O grades at the end of fourth year) often managed to secure
clerical, secretarial and skilled manual jobs.

On a structural level, however, it can be argued that the

tendency for ex-trainees to be concentrated in certain sectors of the labour market does not simply reflect their qualifications but is influenced by the nature of their YTS placement. If we look at young people's occupation or status in autumn 1987 alongside their 1985 YTS placement occupation, it is evident that those initially placed in certain occupations have a better chance of remaining in that occupational field than others. Young people who worked as clerks and secretaries, skilled craftspeople or operatives and labourers whilst on YTS stood a reasonable chance of being employed in a similar occupation in autumn 1987. In these three occupational groups, around a half were employed in the same group in 1987 as they were training in in 1985. In contrast, of those who were placed in personal service or sales occupations, fewer worked in the same sort of occupations in 1987 (33 per cent and 22 per cent respectively).

When the rates of occupational continuity of YTS trainees were compared with the continuity patterns of those in non-YTS employment in 1985,[2] it was clear that those who entered jobs directly were more likely to be working in the same occupational group in autumn 1987. This was true within each occupational group, and occupational continuity among non-trainees was frequently higher by more than a third (Furlong and Raffe, 1989). To a certain extent we would expect to find a lower level of occupational continuity among ex-trainees as, at the end of their time on YTS, those who are not retained by their employers or sponsors must seek employment on the external labour market. (In Chapter 4 I noted that many young people faced difficulties in making the transition from YTS to a job and in Chapter 5 I argued that those who did not move straight from YTS to a job faced great difficulties in escaping from unemployment.) Moreover, because employers tend to favour well-qualified trainees, those who were not retained may be seen as having failed. If we are to judge the value of YTS as an occupational route, the factor which is likely to cause most concern and to lead us to question the value of YTS training is the large proportion of young people who were either unemployed or who had withdrawn from the labour market a couple of years after finishing YTS (see Chapters 5 and 6).

This tendency was particularly problematic in certain occupational groups where a large proportion of ex-trainees were either unemployed or out of the labour market at the age of 19. Of those who trained in personal service occupations, for example, nearly half (49 per cent) were unemployed or out of the labour market in autumn 1987, compared to 16 per cent of those who entered personal service occupations without going through YTS. Similarly, of those trainees placed in sales occupations, 44 per cent were unemployed or out of the labour market in 1987, compared with 18 per cent of direct recruits to sales occupations. In contrast, fewer of those who entered the craft and skilled manual segments of the youth labour market as trainees were unemployed or out of the labour market at this stage (although at 23 per cent it should still cause concern), and the rate of unemployment and labour market withdrawal among ex-trainees was nearly double that of those who entered craft and skilled manual occupations directly.

Once young people become unemployed, their prospects of finding a 'good' job will decrease with the length of their unemployment. When I measured the average job status scores on the Revised Cambridge Scale (Prandy, 1990) of minimum-age school-leavers who were in jobs at the age of 19 (autumn 1987), I found that occupational status fell in relation to total length of unemployment for both males and females (Table 8. 3). The mean Cambridge status score for males with no experience of unemployment was 30·7, compared with 25·9 among those unemployed for a year or more. For females, mean scores among those who had never been unemployed were 42·4 as compared to 34·5 among those who had been out of work for a year or more.[3] Of those working in personal service, sales and unskilled manual jobs, over a half (55 per cent) had experienced unemployment, compared to around a third of those in clerical and skilled manual jobs (34 per cent) and managerial, professional and related jobs (36 per cent).

One of the reasons why protracted periods of unemployment and YTS placements in certain occupations are associated with a decline in status of the jobs young people eventually enter, is that certain employment opportunities are restricted to people of a particular age. For example, well qualified 18-year-olds may be regarded by employers as too old to begin an apprenticeship even if they are willing to accept a low training wage. A similarly qualified school-leaver may be regarded as too young to enter other occupations, such as jobs in security (Ashton *et al.*, 1982 and 1990; Furlong, 1990b).

While the age structure of the job market affected the opportunities available to those trainees who were not retained by their

TABLE 8.3 Cambridge status score of current job*, by total unemployment since leaving school

	Males	Females
No unemployment	30.7	42.4
	(296)	(251)
1–26 weeks	28.9	39.2
	(154)	(125)
27 weeks – 1 year	28.3	34.7
	(50)	(35)
Over 1 year	25 .9	34.5
	(39)	(33)
ANOVA	p = 0.000	p = 0.0009

Note: *Job in autumn 1987, restricted to young people who had entered the labour market by spring 1986.
Unweighted ns are in brackets.

YTS sponsors or employers, ex-trainees were in a somewhat unique position with respect to recruitment. They had undergone a period of work experience and vocational training through which they may have learnt valuable personal or occupational skills; they had 'conformed' by accepting training and may have been perceived positively due to their conformity; they may have avoided prolonged unemployment during a crucial stage in the transition; and, as a result of remaining active in the labour market, they may have developed networks of informal contacts through which they may have subsequently found jobs. As a result of these factors (and because school-leavers who found jobs directly tended to be those with the best qualifications), we would expect ex-trainees and young people with no experience of YTS to undergo different methods of recruitment.

Clearly the occupations in which young people were placed while on YTS were important to their subsequent employment chances (also Lee *et al.*, 1990) and within occupations there were 'good' and 'bad' schemes in respect to retention rates. Overall, around a third of young people said that they were kept on by their YTS employer (33 per cent), while over half of the males (51 per cent) and around four in ten females (39 per cent) said that YTS did not help them to get a job (Table 8. 4).

TABLE 8.4 'In what ways, if any, has being on YTS helped you get a job?', by sex

	Per cent giving as a reason		
	Male	Female	All
YTS has not helped me get a job	51	39	45
I was kept on by my YTS sponsor or employer	31	36	33
My YTS sponsor or supervisor told me about a job with a different employer	2	3	3
I heard about the job through other trainees on the scheme	2	2	2
The certificate or qualification I got on YTS helped me to get a job	8	10	9
I was offered a job because I'd done the same sort of job on YTS	12	16	14
The work experience I got on the scheme helped me to get a job	16	25	20
The skills I learnt on the scheme helped me get a job	14	21	17
I was given a job because I'd been on YTS	7	6	6
I was helped in some other way	12	12	12
Total	155	170	161
Unweighted n	(634)	(581)	(1215)

Note: Percentages do not add to 100 as respondents were able to give more than one reason.

Between these two extremes, young people perceived YTS to have helped them to find jobs in a number of less direct ways often related to what Raffe (1987) has called the 'content' of YTS training. Raffe has argued that only one in nine YTS leavers found a job on the external labour market as a result of the 'content' of YTS. The main indirect ways in which young people saw YTS as helping them find jobs related to the value of the work experience, the skills acquired on the scheme, or being offered a job as a result of having done similar sorts of work while on YTS. Females tended to give these reasons more frequently than males. Qualifications or certificates gained on YTS were mentioned by fewer than one in ten young people (9 per cent). Similarly, YTS was not regarded as an important source of knowledge of vacancies on the external labour market. Very few young people said that they learnt about jobs through informal networks, such as other trainees on the scheme (2 per cent) or through their sponsor or supervisor informing them of vacancies with other firms (3 per cent).

Among the Scottish cohort, around a third of those working in 1987 said that they had found out about their current jobs through family and friends (39 per cent of males and 29 per cent of females): nearly a quarter discovered them through the Jobcentre (22 per cent of males and 27 per cent of females): almost one in five through direct contact with an employer (20 per cent of males and 17 per cent of females): and just over one in ten through press adverts (9 per cent of males and 14 per cent of females) and through YTS (12 per cent of males and 11 per cent of females). Informal contacts such as family and friends were a particularly important source of job discovery among young people in unskilled jobs, of whom almost a half (49 per cent) claimed to have found out about their jobs in this manner. In contrast, only one in five (20 per cent) of those in clerical and secretarial jobs claimed to have discovered their jobs in this way; in other occupations the proportion was around a third.

The other main source of variation in methods of job discovery were that young people (especially females) in clerical and secretarial jobs tended to have discovered their jobs through the Jobcentre, while relatively few young people in unskilled jobs found out about jobs in this manner. Direct contact was important for those in skilled manual jobs and, predictably, shop adverts tended to advertise sales jobs. Young people were also questioned about factors they saw as important in securing their current (1987) jobs. Nearly half (49 per cent) said that they had a 'good interview' for the job. Many also thought that they were given the job due to their qualifications (33 per cent), their training (23 per cent), their work skills (15 per cent) or their previous work experience (24 per cent). Females tended to stress the importance of these training and experience factors to a greater extent than males.

Although many young people said that they had discovered their current job through informal contacts, fewer said that they thought that these contacts were important in securing the job. However, nearly one in five (18 per cent) said that one of the reasons they were given the job was that they were known to the employer, and just over one in ten (12 per cent) said that family contacts were important. Among those in unskilled occupations, young people were more likely to think that family contacts were important in securing the job. Indeed, while 21 per cent of those in unskilled jobs thought family contacts were important, few nurses (6 per cent) clerks and secretaries (4 per cent) or salespeople (6 per cent) regarded family contacts as important. However, more than one in ten managers and professionals (11 per cent), personal service workers (12 per cent) and skilled craftspeople (14 per cent) named family contacts as a reason they thought they were given the job. Over one in five of those in managerial and professional occupations (24 per cent), sales jobs (24 per cent), skilled manual jobs (22 per cent) and personal service jobs thought that one of the reasons they got their jobs was that they were known to the employer.

With a high proportion of school-leavers entering YTS, job entry has become much more complex. Qualifications are still very reliable in predicting the sorts of jobs young men and women will enter, but whether or not a young person enters YTS and if so the sorts of occupation they are trained in, will have an effect on their chances of subsequent employment as well as on their chances of remaining in a similar occupational field. Yet the chances of similarly qualified young people experiencing YTS vary between different parts of the country.

8.3 Local labour markets and recruitment

While both qualifications and post-16 experiences are important in explaining the ways in which occupational entry is structured, it is also important to take account of variations within local labour markets which influence the recruitment process. Young people's opportunities are affected by the occupational and industrial structure of the area in which they live and this has an impact on their chances of avoiding unemployment, their chances of finding work without joining schemes, and the sorts of full-time jobs they eventually enter. Levels of all-age unemployment within a labour market and the level of YTS, participation both effect the risk of personal unemployment (Chapter 5). Furthermore, the social composition of an area is related directly to young people's school performance and the sorts of educational expectations which are generated in certain cultural environments. Hence, young people's chances of participating in post-compulsory education is likely to vary from one area to another.

Within Scotland there is a large variation in the social composition of areas:[4] in Glasgow, for example, 15 per cent of young people in the cohort had fathers working in managerial, professional and related occupations as compared to 33 per cent in Lothian. In Grampian, Lothian and Borders, fewer than one in twenty had fathers who were unemployed or in part-time jobs, compared with one in five in Glasgow. These differences in the social composition of areas were reflected in young people's educational attainments: in Glasgow nearly half (48 per cent) had no O grade passes by the end of the fourth year of secondary schooling, while in Grampian, Highlands and Islands, Tayside, Lothian, Renfrew and Dumbarton, less than a third completed their fourth year of secondary schooling without passing an O grade. Another study, that of Garner and colleagues (1988) found a substantial variation in the education and employment chances of comparable school-leavers across the four Scottish cities (Edinburgh, Glasgow, Aberdeen and Dundee). Moreover, they argued that these differences were not merely derivative of other inequalities such as social class, but were important in their own right. In England Ashton and colleagues (1988) have also emphasised the importance of local labour market characteristics for an understanding of transitional processes.

In autumn 1987, levels of unemployment among the Scottish cohort were lowest in Grampian and Borders (7 per cent and 8 per cent respectively) and highest in Glasgow and Lanark (24 per cent and 22 per cent respectively). Patterns of employment mirrored the incidence of unemployment and areas with the highest levels of youth unemployment, (Glasgow and Lanark) had the lowest proportion of young people in full-time jobs (both 49 per cent) while Grampian and the Borders (with the lowest levels of youth unemployment) had the highest employment rates (69 per cent and 71 per cent respectively).

Other work on the cohort has shown that the local unemployment rate had an important effect on school-leaving rates and that fewer 16-year-olds left school in areas of high unemployment (Raffe and Willms, 1989). Raffe and Willms suggest that this 'discouraged worker' effect was strongest among 16 year-olds with attainments slightly above average who may have been on the margins of deciding whether to stay on at school (there is evidence that the 'discouraged worker' effect is specific to Scotland, see Chapter 2). Areas with high levels of unemployment also tended to have low proportions of young people in full-time education in autumn 1987; this probably reflects the social composition of these areas. The highest rate of educational participation in autumn 1987 was found among young people in Lothian, followed by Tayside and Renfrew.

Across Scotland there was a considerable variation in the sorts of jobs entered by young people. In Renfrew, for example, 35 per cent of young workers were employed in clerical and secretarial occupations, while in Borders and Tayside only 14 per cent of young people worked in these occupations. 8 per cent of young workers in the Borders worked in sales and personal service occupations, compared with 32 per cent in Tayside. In the Borders, 51 per cent of young workers were employed as operatives and labourers, as compared to just 17 per cent in Highlands and Islands and Dumbarton (Furlong, 1991).

Regional variation in the level of employment and in the occupational and industrial structure of an area affects the availability of training opportunities. In Grampian more than four in ten males had been apprenticed at some stage, while in Dumfries an Galloway, Lothian, Ayr, Renfrew and Glasgow, fewer than one in four had been apprenticed. Areas with a large service sector and white-collar workforce tend inevitably to have a lower apprentice intake than areas with a large manufacturing sector.

Training opportunities through YTS were found to vary regionally, as were the chances of young people being employed subsequently by their YTS sponsor or employer. In Glasgow and Lanark, over half the cohort experienced YTS, while in Grampian, Highlands and Islands and Lothian, less than a third had experience of YTS. Chances of being employed by one's YTS employer or sponsor varied from 60 per cent in the Borders to 23 per cent in Dumfries and Galloway.

The pattern of differences between areas is complex and our discussion so far has revealed few clear and simple correlations between the relative strengths of the various influences on young people's post-16 experiences. Areas with high rates of unemployment, for example, may have a predominance of declining industries and of people with certain social characteristics. As yet we cannot say which of these factors has the greatest effect. In the next part of this chapter I will attempt to clarify this by highlighting the relative strengths of various factors in predicting employment probability and job status among 19-year-olds.

8. 4 Predicting employment and job status

In order to examine the importance of the various factors within the local labour market which may influence young people's post-school opportunities, multivariate analysis was used. An attempt was made to assess the significance of the different aspects of local opportunity structures in predicting whether young people would be employed in autumn 1987 and, if so, their occupational status on the Cambridge occupational status scale.[5]

With respect to young people's chances of being in employment, the analysis confirmed that school and vocational qualifications increased young people's chances of being in employment to a greater extent than the occupational and industrial structure of the local labour market. Young people who had experienced YTS were less likely to be employed than those without such experience, although this may well reflect the effects of a period of unemployment before or immediately after YTS (as discussed in Chapter 5). In terms of local area factors, the all-age unemployment rate tended to be a strong local area predictor of employment probability.[6] There was little clear indication that the local occupational and industrial structure was affecting employment probability independently of the local unemployment rate.

While employment probability tells us something about the level of opportunities within an area, it tells us nothing about the quality of such opportunities. To rectify this shortcoming I conducted a further multivariate analysis[7] to predict the Revised Cambridge Status Score (Prandy, 1990) of the occupations of males and females in full-time jobs in autumn 1987 in order to assess the influence of the local labour market on occupational status. This analysis confirmed the importance of school qualifications; the number of O grade passes achieved was associated with a higher status score. In terms of local factors, areas with high levels of all-age unemployment tended to be associated with a reduction in the status of occupations entered by females. This was significant even after controlling for the occupational and industrial structure of the area. For males the relationship between local all-age unemployment and occupational status was not significant, although this may reflect a narrower status spread of occupations entered by males who left school at the minimum age. Females were more likely than males to have entered service sector industries, and for them a high proportion of local employment in service sector industries was associated with an increase in occupational status.

In sum, it can be argued that variation in young people's employment experiences within different local areas are most strongly influenced by the local all-age unemployment rate rather than by differences in the occupational or industrial structure of the area.

8. 5 Conclusion

The routes young people follow into the labour market tend to be determined by social class and school attainments, but there is also evidence to suggest that post-16 experiences can affect young people's occupational opportunities. The evidence discussed in this chapter reinforces the earlier conclusions about YTS: for many young people it is an extremely risky route. Those who join YTS often find it difficult obtain employment within the same segment of the labour market, and when they do make a 'successful' transition into the world of work they often find that the sorts of jobs entered bear little relation to their YTS 'training' (see also Lee *et al.*, 1990).

To an extent it can be argued that YTS represents the 'disadvantaged' route from school to work, embarked on by young people from disadvantaged backgrounds with below-average school qualifications. But YTS reinforces these inequalities by placing young people in high-risk sectors of the economy and in occupations where few will subsequently find employment. Unemployment rates are extremely high among young people 'trained' in occupations like sales and personal service, and the longer they remain unemployed the greater chance they have of entering low-status, unskilled jobs. Indeed, for those who 'train' in personal service and sales jobs and subsequently enter semi- and unskilled manual jobs, YTS can be regarded as little more than a 'holding device' in which young people are removed from the unemployment register until they reach the age at which employers will consider them for unskilled manual jobs within the 'adult' labour market. These factors must lead to a questioning of the value of YTS and hence the value of Youth Training for a large proportion of young people.

Notes

1. Details of pre-entry experiences and qualifications are taken from Furlong and Raffe (1989).
2. The record of occupational continuity among ex-YTS trainees is likely to be understated as a result of some trainees with 'employee status' being unaware that they were on YTS. Those with employee status have far greater security than ordinary trainees and where they are classified as 'employees' rather than 'trainees', this will give an over-pessimistic view of the record of YTS.
3. Higher average Cambridge status scores for females reflects the higher status allocated to white-collar and service-type occupations.
4. The areas used in this chapter are based on the Scottish Local Enterprise Company (LEC) areas. Due to small sample numbers, the LECs within the Highlands and Islands Development Board (HIDB) area have been treated as a single unit and are described in the text as 'Highlands'. Young people were allocated to LEC areas on the basis of the last secondary school attended or current residence in autumn 1987.
5. See Appendix II for a full description of the multivariate analysis.
6. The effect of local unemployment is partly diluted by the inclusion of the variable measuring YTS experience and proportion of minimum-age school-leavers in a Travel-To-Work Area. These variables may act as a proxy for unemployment and thus reduce its apparent significance.
7. See Appendix II for full description of multivariate analysis.

9
TRANSITIONS AND LIFE STYLES

9. 1 Introduction

Studies of the youth transition have tended to concentrate *either* on the development of young people as workers and on the reproduction of social inequalities based on class and gender, *or* on social and psychological aspects of the transition from youth to adulthood. In this book I have concentrated on the former, but I am aware of the importance of locating a study of the transition from school to work within the broader social psychological context of the transition from adolescence to adulthood. In this chapter I will consider some other aspects of the transition from school and examine the development of distinctive life-styles among young people during the transitional stage. Consideration of this dimension of the transition can help inform our thinking about the ways in which social inequalities are reproduced.

I look first at the emergence of differential leisure patterns during the transition; work and leisure are closely related, and an understanding of these two key aspects of social life are important in any evaluation of the quality of life enjoyed by young people. Second, I focus on patterns of leaving home as a central feature of the transition to adulthood. Finally, in order to try and reconcile sociological and psychological perspectives, I look at the ways in which the transition may be portrayed as a stressful period in young people's lives by examining the effects of different transitional experiences on young people's mental health.

9. 2 Transitional experiences and leisure patterns[1]

Throughout adolescence, young people develop distinctive views and expectations about the relationship between work and leisure and different approaches to the use of time which is free from other obligations. These patterns tend to be reinforced in adult life.

Leisure is usually defined as time which is free from other commitments: time over which a person can exercise a degree of choice and control (Roberts, 1983). However, by defining leisure

as time in which 'free choice' is exercised, there is a danger of
losing sight of the ways in which leisure life-styles are structured
through our differential experiences within the social structure.
Work and leisure are two sides of the one coin; the meaning of one
is dependent on the meaning of the other. Those engaged in work
which they find boring, from which they gain little intrinsic satisfaction, may regard work instrumentally and come to see leisure
as a form of compensation. In this context, work becomes a means
of providing the resources through which a person can gain
pleasure and satisfaction outside of the work environment. In
contrast, those following middle-class careers may find features
of their working lives inherently satisfying and the distinction
between work and leisure may be blurred; a sociologist, for example, may spend part of their 'leisure' time reading academic books
for personal enjoyment. The ways in which leisure time is spent
may enhance the quality of life, but for many professional workers it is inappropriate to regard leisure as compensation for the
deprivations of working life.

In terms of the youth transition, it is important to examine the
differences in leisure life-styles of young men and women and to
look at the ways in which work and educational experiences
during the transitional period influence the emergence of distinctive life-styles which reflect class and gender differences. Class
differences in leisure are conditioned by cultural beliefs and dis-
positions as well as by differential access to resources which make
rich and varied use of free time possible. Members of the middle
classes, who tend to follow more satisfying careers, often engage
in the broadest range of leisure-time pursuits. In contrast, working-class leisure is often narrower and more 'passive', with
people spending more of their time being entertained by watching TV and spectator sports (Roberts, 1983).

Gender differences in leisure are more strongly defined than
class differences and this must be understood as part of the process of gender socialisation which begins at birth. As a result of this
process women are often expected, and come to expect, that they
will participate in the sorts of leisure activities which are considered appropriate for women and which are compatible with
established feminine roles (Clarke and Critcher, 1985). Clarke and
Critcher argue that gender differences in society are expressed
and validated through leisure. In sport, for example, women
are often confined to those activities which do not put their

femininity 'at risk'. In sports which attract both men and women, gender segregation serves to portray women as unfit to compete with men, thus 'sport at all levels converts physical differences into cultural definitions of superiority and inferiority ensuring that women come off second best' (Clarke and Critcher, 1985, pp. 162). Men are more likely than women to spend their leisure time engaged in active pursuits outside the home environment, for example, playing and watching sports or visiting the 'Pub'. Women, on the other hand (and especially women with children) tend to engage in more passive and home-centred activities: watching TV; visiting friends and relations; and going out for meals (Roberts *et al.*, 1990; Rapoport and Rapoport, 1975)

These class and gender differences in leisure patterns develop during adolescence and become established through young people's transitional experiences. By the age of 19, young people's leisure patterns show a considerable variation which reflects their future class positions. Those who remain in full-time education after the minimum leaving age (many of whom will occupy advantaged positions within the labour market) tend to participate in the greatest range of leisure activities and organised groups. The unemployed take part in fewer activities and are members of fewer organised groups than either students and workers. Young workers tend to go out more often during the evening than either students or the unemployed (Roberts *et al.*, 1990).

In order to make a broader comparative study of the leisure experiences of students, workers and the unemployed, Roberts, Campbell and Furlong (1990) produced summary scores to measure the number of leisure activities mentioned by young people and the frequency with which they participated in them, the breadth of their social networks and the number of organised groups in which they participated. On each of these three indices, the students achieved the highest scores: they took part in a greater range of activities; mixed with a greater variety of people, and took part in more organised groups than those who were in jobs or unemployed. Those who were working achieved higher scores than the unemployed on the leisure activity scale and the group membership scale, but young people who were in jobs and unemployed achieved the same rating on the social network scale. The social inequalities which structured post-16 experiences in education and the labour market permeated much of young people's social existence. Leisure life-styles varied according to labour market status and these differences were structured as a result of transitional experiences and social class. Those who experienced post-compulsory education enhanced both their future career prospects and their future leisure life-styles. Roberts, Campbell and Furlong compared the leisure patterns at age 19 of minimum-age school-leavers and young people who had completed one or two post-compulsory years at school. They found that those who delayed leaving education had richer leisure patterns, irrespective of their labour market status at age 19, achieving higher scores on each of the three summary measures of leisure participation.

Although post-compulsory education did not protect young people from the effects of subsequent unemployment, the leisure advantages of extended education were obvious whether individuals were employed or unemployed. This implies that leisure patterns associated with extended education are retained after young people enter the labour force. However, the leisure patterns associated with continued education did not extend to trainees on YTS. When current status was controlled for, young people who had no experience of YTS achieved higher scores on all three summary measures of leisure activity. Just as participation in post-compulsory education was found to confer advantages for future leisure participation among young adults, it was discovered that the effects of unemployment in reducing leisure scores were evident among young people who had subsequently returned to full-time education or found work.

Cultural differences and resource inequalities among young people from different classes mean that we can expect to find distinct leisure life-styles among people located in different parts of the occupational structure. Ashton and Field (1976), for example, argued that those who entered unskilled jobs often regarded work as an uncongenial and unsatisfying feature of life which supplied the material resources for enjoyment of leisure time. It was argued that these young people tended to do most of their living off-the-job. In contrast, those who had entered jobs with some career structure (including apprenticeships) often gained pleasure through work achievements. In this sense, leisure activities could be seen as providing extra satisfactions.

If it is true that those who work in monotonous jobs expect to gain compensation outside of the work environment, then we would expect them to enjoy particularly active lives outside the working day. If this is not the case it could be argued that work inequalities are reinforced in the leisure sphere. In order to examine the variation in leisure patterns amongst those in different jobs, Furlong, Campbell and Roberts (1990) divided occupations into two categories referred to as 'reasonable' jobs and 'lowskill' jobs.[2] In terms of leisure activity, social networks, group membership and number of evenings out, those in 'reasonable' jobs had higher scores than those in 'low skill' jobs. The relationship was similar for males and females. This suggests that young people in dead-end jobs do not gain any recompense for the alienating nature of their work through out-of-work activities.

9. 3 Transitional experiences and home leaving[3]

As the transition from school to work has become more protracted, as much of the youth labour market has been subsumed into YTS, and as eligibility for various benefits has been restricted so as to exclude the majority of young people, it has become increasingly difficult for young people to make the transition to adulthood by setting up their own homes. While young people are living with their parents, to an extent they remain under parental control; they must abide by the 'house rules' and consequently tend not to have their adult status fully recognised until they leave the family home (Leonard, 1980; Hutson and Jenkins, 1987).

These changes have affected some groups of young people more severely than others: those following routes into the labour market which include higher education are least affected because students often have access to low-cost housing (although a decline in the real value of student grants and withdrawal of housing benefits may encourage some to apply to a local university or college); the unemployed and YTS trainees face great difficulties in leaving home owing to their lack of resources and the withdrawal of support to young householders. Once they have found a non-YTS job, young workers who are paid enough to able to support themselves face fewer difficulties, although the removal of benefit safety nets may discourage them from moving to a new area in search of work.

According to data from the 1981 National Child Development Study, 65 per cent of men and 84 per cent of women had left home by the age of 23; among those who had left home by the age of 23, the median leaving age was 21·9 years for men and 20 for women

(Jones, 1987). Among the Scottish cohort, 28 per cent of respondents reported that they had left home by the age of 19. Those who had left home at this stage tended to be the best qualified young people who were predominantly from middle-class family backgrounds (Jones, 1987b; Furlong and Cooney, 1990). Females were more likely than males to have left home because they tend to marry at a younger age than males and because they tend to remain in education longer than males and thus were more likely to leave home to go to university or college.

Furlong and Cooney (1990) found that members of the Scottish cohort who had left home could be placed into one of four categories: those who left to continue their education (34 per cent); those who left to start a particular job or in order to look for work in another area (29 per cent); those who left because they were getting married or because they wished to set up their own home (22 per cent); and those who left because of problems getting on with people at home (16 per cent). Those who left home to continue their education were the best qualified (93 per cent had four or more O grades), were most likely to be females (59 per cent) and tended to come from middle-class families (55 per cent had fathers in Registrar General's classes I and II). Young people who left home in order to look for work or to take up the offer of a job were also reasonably well qualified; 47 per cent had four or more O grades and a further 28 per cent had between one and three O grades. In terms of social class, those who left for work-related reasons were not as socially concentrated as those who left for educational reasons (32 per cent had fathers in class I and II). Young people who left in order to set up their own home or because of problems in the parental home had fewest qualifications (43 per cent of those who left to set up their own homes and 54 per cent of those who left home due to problems had no O grade passes). More than two-thirds were female (71 per cent and 67 per cent respectively) and relatively few had middle-class fathers (14 per cent and 13 per cent respectively).

In many respects, Government policies towards youth over the last decade have been contradictory; young people were urged to 'get on their bikes' in order to find work in other areas, while benefits were withdrawn from those who followed this advice. Policy has tended to be based on the view that the state should not be placed in a position of having to subsidise young people who leave home, as this is regarded as the responsibility of the family.

Despite the Government's suspicion that benefits were being abused by young people seeking a quick route to independence, Furlong and Cooney (1990) found little evidence to support this view among members of the Scottish cohort who left home for reasons other than education. Unemployment among those who left home for work-related reasons was significantly lower than among those who stayed at home, and job occupancy was higher. This needs interpreting cautiously. Although it would appear that those who moved away from home for work reduced their chances of unemployment, members of this group had above-average qualifications and had advantages in terms of social class. When the unemployment rate among young people with four or more O grades who left home for work was compared with the unemployment rate among similarly qualified young people who stayed at home, the rate was found to be the same (5 per cent).

However, those who left the family home in order to set up their own home or due to problems at home were found to be vulnerable to unemployment and had a low level of job occupancy (many of the females were working full-time in the home). Yet the high level of unemployment reflected the composition of the group which was skewed towards lower qualified, lower social class females who tend to marry and have children at a relatively early age. Among the young workers who had left home, twice as many were working in managerial, professional and related occupations than among those who had remained at home. Many of those who had left home had joined one of the Armed Forces and a high proportion were to be found in personal service occupations (especially females).

What is often the final stage of the youth transition, leaving the family home, needs to be understood in relation to the broader transitional process. It is an element of the structure of the transition, and the stage at which young people leave home is dependent on the route they have been following from school, on the conditions prevalent in the labour market, and on current social legislation. Fears that the availability of benefits will encourage young people to leave home before they are fully able to support themselves are unfounded; young people who leave home for reasons other than education tend to enter fairly desirable jobs for which young workers are often required to move away from the family home. Levels of unemployment among those who left home were not significantly different from those among comparable groups of young people who remained at home. However, the lack of an adequate benefit safety net may deter some young people from leaving home for jobs in other areas and thus obstruct labour mobility.

9. 4 Transitional experiences and mental health

In Chapter 1 I suggested that sociologists had come to regard the transition as a relatively smooth process because outcomes tended to confirm prior expectations. Yet the increased protraction of the transition from school, widespread unemployment and uncertainty makes it more difficult to characterise the transition as stable and predictable. In order to conclude the empirical examination of the transition from school I will consider the extent to which young people following different post-16 routes found their transition to be hard going.[4]

Throughout this book I have argued that the transition from school to work has remained a highly structured and predictable process: young people from certain backgrounds and with particular qualifications are differentially channelled through a series of experiences which on the surface appear to offer a variety of new opportunities to young people who have the 'right' attitude and are willing to invest their time and energy in developing their skills. However, although social scientists may depict transitional outcomes as structured and predictable, for young people outcomes appear less certain. They tend to be unsure about whether they will achieve their objectives or whether they will have to settle for less desirable alternatives. For many, the time spent on YTS will be a time of uncertainty and any time spent unemployed will tend to be experienced as stressful.

Ashton and Field (1976) have argued that when young people's early expectations are confirmed at work, the transition from school can be regarded as being a relatively trouble-free period. Young people from lower working-class families tend to have few expectations of personal fulfilment at work and approach their work in an instrumental manner. In contrast, young people from middle-class homes often expect to gain personal fulfilment through their work. However, Ashton and Field recognised that the transition could be particularly difficult when early expectations and work realities came into conflict. This could occur, for example, when young people who had worked hard at school and emerged with 'good' qualifications and expectations of a

TABLE 9.1 Mean GHQ scores, by current status

	Male	Female	All
Youth Training Scheme	0.69	0.70	0.70
Full-time job	0.71	0.76	0.74
Unemployed	1.06	1.19	1.12
Full-time education	0.83	0.96	0.90
Full-time work in the home	*	(1.09)	(1.07)
Other	(0.75)	0.95	0.87
ANOVA	p=0.001	p=0.001	p=0.001

Notes: *Denotes a cell with a base n less than 20.
Brackets denote a base n of less than 50.

fulfilling job subsequently found themselves working on the shop-floor alongside people with no qualifications and with different cultural values.

In the 1970s such cases were seen as the exception to the general rule of congruent experiences. With the decline in jobs for young people and increases in unemployment it became more common for young people to enter situations where their expectations conflicted with their subsequent experiences (Furlong, 1987; 1988a). Experience of unemployment has become common for school-leavers in some areas (Ashton *et al.*, 1982; Roberts *et al.*, 1982; Chapter 8), and as a result of the shortage of jobs many young people have had to accept jobs which they find unfulfilling. Consequently it is important to discover whether young people who are unemployed or those with above-average qualifications working in low-skill jobs experienced a difficult transition. To achieve this, Furlong and Spearman (1989) measured the 'psychological well-being' or 'mental health' of members of the Scottish cohort at age 17 (spring 1986), and made comparisons between young people in different situations. In order to measure psychological well-being, they used a scale derived from the twelve-item General Health Questionnaire (GHQ).[5] Being a self-administered test, the GHQ lends itself well to inclusion in postal surveys. However, as the GHQ was only administered on one occasion we should not try to draw causal inferences. The GHQ is a self-administered screening test which is often used to measure general levels of psychological distress and to detect psychiatric disorders of a non-psychotic nature (Goldberg, 1972; Banks and Ullah, 1988).

Furlong and Spearman (1989) found that those who were unemployed at age 17 had the poorest psychological well-being (having the highest GHQ scores) (Table 9. 1) while there was no significant difference between those on YTS and those in jobs.

Within each status group, but especially among the unemployed, females were found to have lower levels of psychological well-being. Females who described themselves as working in the home were also found to have poor levels of psychological well-being (similar to males who were unemployed). In Chapter 6 I suggested that there was a link between women's unemployment and labour market withdrawal; Furlong and Spearman's analysis suggests that withdrawing from the labour market is likely to bring them little benefit in terms of psychological well-being.

The differences in levels of psychological well-being were broadly in line with what we would have expected through knowledge of the sociological work on the transition. School-leavers who had failed to make a 'successful' transition by finding jobs or schemes were suffering the difficult effects of incongruence between early expectation (of a job) and the reality (of unemployment). As those who were unemployed tended to suffer in terms of mental health they could be said to be experiencing a difficult transition. However, the effect of unemployment on psychological well-being did not have a lasting effect once a young person had secured a job (Chapter 5). Although the unemployed displayed measures of psychological well-being which were significantly worse than those in work or on YTS, Furlong and Spearman were concerned that there may have been important differences among those in jobs which reflect transitional experiences: in other words, that young people who had invested time and energy in their school work and had emerged with above-average qualifications would be particularly vulnerable if they subsequently found work in an unskilled capacity (Ashton and Field, 1976). With a general decline in the availability of apprenticeships and 'respectable' jobs, this scenario has become increasingly likely (Chapter 3). To test this hypothesis, GHQ scores were examined in relation to the sorts of jobs young people obtained and the number of SCEs gained at the end of the fourth year at school. Jobs were grouped into two broad categories: clerical, skilled manual and higher level; and semi- and unskilled jobs and shop work. It was found that those with above-average qualifications who were employed in low-skill jobs had levels of psychological well-being which were substantially worse than those with similar qualifications in clerical, skilled or higher-level occupations. However, for most young people any job would appear to be better than no job; those who left school with 'good' qualifications and subsequently entered low-skill jobs had higher-levels of psychological well-being than those who were unemployed.

9. 5 Conclusion

Analysis of young people's transition from school to work is important to an understanding of occupational placement and social reproduction, and I have argued that the process is structured through social class and educational achievements. The study of the youth transition can also illuminate many other areas of young people's social existence. Distinctive patterns of use of non-work time can be identified and I have argued that those disadvantaged in occupational terms by working in jobs which offer low remuneration and few intrinsic rewards tend not to gain compensation for these deprivations through a rich or varied social existence. The transition to an independent life outside the family is structured by social class and educational achievements. Again, those with social and educational advantages are able to leave home at an earlier age and with fewer risks than those who are less advantaged.

In many ways, the transition from school to work in the 1980s and 1990s is as predictable as in the 1960s and 1970s. There have been a number of changes which have affected young people's experiences of the transition, but there are also many elements of continuity. In so far as occupational outcomes are structured and predictable and represent a 'congruence' of experience for young people, it could be argued that the transition from school to work is still, in general, a routine process. Yet the analysis of young people's psychological well-being shows that subjective interpretations of the transition do not reflect the smoothness of the transition on an objective level.

Typically, young people hope to enter higher-level jobs than they eventually achieve; this was the case in the 1960s and 1970s

(Carter, 1962) and is the same today. Subjective aspirations become 'cooled-out' through experience within objective labour market structures. In addition, in the 1980s and 1990s, many young people experienced post-school and post-YTS unemployment. Others were forced to modify occupational aspirations which had been reinforced on YTS as they found a lack of 'suitable' vacancies in the labour market. For these young people, the transition from school is likely to be experienced as a difficult period in their lives.

Notes

1. This section draws on analysis carried out in collaboration with Ken Roberts and Rosie Campbell.
2. Jobs such as managerial, professional, technical, clerical work and skilled manual jobs were classified as 'reasonable' jobs and jobs such as semi- and unskilled manual work and routine sales jobs as 'low skill'.
3. This section draws on analysis carried out in collaboration with George Cooney.
4. This section draws on analysis carried out in collaboration with Michael Spearman.
5. The GHQ which is central to this paper was included in only one version, so in effect we are concentrating on 50 per cent of the cohort. In numerical terms, 2,481 young people completed the GHQ questions. Ethnic minority groups in Scotland are relatively small, so this is largely a study of young white men and women. Responses were weighted by gender, level of attainment and stage of leaving school to population figures provided by the Scottish Examination Board and the Scottish Education Department in order to compensate for differential response rates. Scale values were obtained from the GHQ by coding the responses to each question from 0 to 3 (0 being the most positive response and 3 the most negative). The scores for each of the twelve questions were then added and divided by twelve. }

10
CONCLUSION

For many young people, the transition from school to work can be regarded as a difficult period in their lives. The increased protraction of the transition over recent years has certainly made the transition more difficult than it was during the 1960s and 1970s. Few young people these days will manage to avoid a stressful experience during the transition: becoming unemployed, enduring the uncertainty of a scheme or having to make downward adjustments to their occupational aspirations. This is especially true of young people from working-class homes who leave school with few qualifications, although even those who remain in post-compulsory education must endure periods of uncertainty as they await examination results and as they wait to discover if they have gained entrance to college or university.

Difficult transitions are not simply the result of the increased protraction: the transition from school to work has *never* been an easy process. To the detached observer, the outcomes of the transition are just as predictable today as they were twenty years ago: we can predict which sort of person will pass exams; the type of person who will experience prolonged and repeated periods of unemployment; who will find jobs at the end of their time on youth training schemes; and what sort of jobs young people with various qualifications and experiences will enter.

On an objective level the predictability of the transition has not changed. The situation today is much the same today as it was when Ashton and Field described it in the 1970s. Young people from working-class families follow trajectories which take them through the lower streams at school towards the less skilled positions within the labour market. Those from middle-class families follow trajectories which take them through the higher streams at school towards skilled positions within the labour market. However, Ashton and Field overlooked the subjective uncertainty of the process by presenting a somewhat 'oversocialised' picture of youth. The process of socialisation in the home and the school is not sufficiently strong to ensure that young people's subjective interpretations reflect the objective realities of the labour market. The dominant feature of the transition for young people is uncertainty: this was true in the 1960s (Carter, 1962) and remains true today. Young people tend to leave school hoping for higher level jobs than those which they are likely to achieve, and subjective orientations are only brought into line with the objective socio-economic structure through experiences in the labour market: their aspirations are 'cooled-out' until they reflect the structure of opportunities available to them.

One of the main questions I set out to answer in this book was whether the new transition, with its greater protraction and range of experiences, has resulted in new opportunities for young people and hence changed the nature of the transition from school to work. While clearly new opportunities have been created which some individuals may benefit from, on a social level the effects of the changes on the opportunity structure have been, at best, superficial. Despite a general improvement in qualifications, and despite a greater proportion of young people participating in post-16 education and training and investment in vocational education, family background has remained a strong determinant of educational 'success'. The 'new vocationalism' has so far failed to reduce class- and gender-based inequalities in education and training.

Over the last decade there have been many changes in the transition from school to work. Unemployment and scheme participation are now common, and despite a reduction in unemployment in the South East of England, in much of Scotland, Wales, Northern Ireland and in many parts of England, youth unemployment has shown little sign of disappearing.

By concentrating on the changes in the transition, there is a tendency to lose sight of the similarities: there are still clear and predictable routes from school to work in which those who are advantaged in social and educational terms come to enter the most prestigious and well-paid segments of the labour market. Unemployment and schemes are experiences largely reserved for those following 'disadvantaged' routes into the labour market. Although qualified school-leavers sometimes experience schemes, the stratification of youth training means that their experiences are quite different to those of unqualified school-leavers.

Training schemes carry their own risks which can severely affect young people's experience of the transition and their future life chances. I have argued that processes of socialisation in the home and the school are not powerful enough to ensure that young people leave school with aspirations focused towards the narrow band of occupations available to them in the labour market. Young people from lower working-class families do not actively seek unskilled work as part of their rejection of the middle-class values embodied in the school or as a celebration of working-class culture. Prior to the introduction of youth schemes, young people were forced to reconcile their occupational aspirations with the opportunities available in the local labour market fairly soon after leaving school. Schemes make it possible for young people to retain aspirations which are 'unrealistic' in terms of local demand and may serve to shore-up these aspirations. This can result in a more difficult transition as young people are forced to abandon occupational self-concepts in which they have invested whilst on schemes.

The risks from schemes are not confined to the psychological sphere as participation can have a negative effect on future labour market biographies. Experience of YTS certainly provided no compensation for social and educational disadvantages, and those who succeeded in finding work after YTS tended to be those who were already advantaged prior to joining. Those who failed to move straight from YTS to a job were particularly vulnerable to prolonged unemployment. It is true that YTS experience could help reduce personal chances of unemployment, but this must be judged in the context of individual trajectories. Young people with few qualifications, those in areas of high unemployment and those who 'trained' in sales or personal service occupations were likely to derive few advantages from YTS: they often took up employment in different occupations to those for which they had trained, and if they were unsuccessful in finding work straight after their schemes they often found themselves labelled as 'double failures'.

The effects of unemployment on young people's trajectories can be devastating: many of those who became unemployed encountered extreme difficulties in making their escape into the world of work. Among the Scottish cohort, in any six-month period, little more than one in five young people managed to escape from the clutches of unemployment. Yet the incidence of unemployment is highly structured and reflects social and educational disadvantage: among 19-year-olds around a quarter of those who were unemployed had a father who was unemployed or unable to work. Some young people, especially young women, found that the only way to escape unemployment was to withdraw from the labour market.

An enduring feature of the transition from school to work is the way routes continue to be stratified along gender lines: despite an increase in qualifications among females at school, young women still follow different educational courses, are trained in different areas whilst on schemes and are routed into traditional 'female' segments of the labour market with lower levels of remuneration and fewer prospects for career advancement. Changes in the nature of the transition have not altered the structure of opportunities for young women.

The sorts of jobs young people eventually enter reflect their social background and educational achievements: the expansion of post-16 education and training has resulted in few new opportunities, but the protracted transition carries many new risks. Young people with few qualifications tend to be drafted on to schemes in the 'high risk' sectors of the labour market where they are vulnerable to post-scheme unemployment; in turn unemployment reduces their chances of obtaining a job requiring a reasonable level of skill.

From a social policy perspective, Government intervention and the billions of pounds spent on training schemes have achieved virtually nothing beyond the provision of an alternative to the dole. Indeed, one of the few benefits of youth training schemes identified by David Ashton and colleagues (1990) was the way schemes helped to structure the time of young people who would otherwise be unemployed.

Over the last decade there has been an overall decline in semi- and unskilled manual jobs available to school-leavers, together with a decrease in opportunities for gaining traditional craft skills (Ashton *et al.*, 1990; Chapter 3). At the same time, there has been an increasing tendency for young people to participate in post-compulsory education and training, coupled with a vocationalisation of the curriculum for 'lower ability' pupils. Despite this evidence of a willingness to invest in their own training, little progress has been made towards the development of a highly skilled youth labour force which would enable Britain to compete in European and overseas markets during the next decade and into the twenty-first century. Indeed, the Youth Training Scheme, which until recently was the major form of training available to almost half of the school-leavers in Britain, has done little to reduce Britain's overstocked pool of unskilled labour. The adoption of YTS as the Government's preferred policy option pre-empted the development of other training initiatives which may have tackled the problem more successfully.

It is true that much of this critique would now be accepted by the Government who would argue that the introduction of Youth Training (YT) brings a new flexibility into training and overcomes many of the limitations of YTS. Yet many of the differences be-tween YT and YTS may be regarded as superficial: a cynic may argue that the 'new' scheme is an attempt to move the goal posts so as to avoid criticism which would damage the credibility of the schemes. Since the mid-1970s a number of 'new' schemes have been introduced, partly as a result of bad publicity and a lack of confidence among the consumers towards the previous scheme. However, few of these 'reforms' have represented a significant advance (Lee *et al.*, 1990) and there is little reason to believe that YT will succeed where YTS has failed.

While Government policy has failed to provide adequate solu-tions, employers must also take a share of the blame for the current state of affairs and for the shortage of skilled workers. Employers have been quick to criticise any perceived fall in edu-cational standards and any lack of scientific and technical skills among young workers, yet they have devalued technical educa-tion by continuing to show a preference for school-leavers with 'traditional' qualifications in their recruitment practices. They have also been slow to accept any responsibility for developing the skills of the workforce from which they would eventually profit. They have been guilty of enhancing the short-term profit-ability of their firms by exploiting trainees, providing a bare mini-mum of training and 'employing' a constant stream of trainees rather than building up their permanent workforces.

In an unregulated capitalist economy firms will continue to maximise profits rather than develop the potential of workers. In the age of global capitalism, companies will seek skills on the international market, sometimes using cheap, Third World, la-bour or relocating in advanced societies to take advantage of a technically competent workforce. It is the Government's job to maintain employment levels in Britain by providing the conditions which will ensure the workforce is able to compete at the highest level in terms of skills and services. And it is the Government who are responsible for developing the skills of tomorrow's citizens which will enable them to fulfil their own potential inside and outside the work environment. If these aims are to be met, both Government and educationalists need to move forward with an awareness of the need to enhance and equalise the position of women in the labour force and in society in general. In this respect, as in others, training schemes have offered potential but have been a wasted opportunity. Without active intervention employers are likely to continue with the old discriminatory practices.

Although the current situation is partly the result of policies followed by employers and the Department of Employment, some of the blame must also be placed with educationalists. While imaginative curricula developments have been devised, such as the Scottish Action Plan, schools and universities have continued to hold 'traditional' academic subjects in highest esteem whilst regarding vocational education as suitable only for those who lack the ability to succeed in conventional subjects. Educationalists have been aware for many years that a large proportion of working-class children find the school environment and curriculum alienating, either rejecting the values of the school (Jackson and Marsden, 1962; Hargreaves, 1967; Willis, 1977) or at best regarding the school in instrumental terms as a means of getting the qualifications required to succeed in the labour market (Brown, 1987b). Yet in policy terms, educationalists have failed to respond effectively to the situation.

In some respects, sociologists have legitimised this inaction. Paul Willis in particular, has given credence to the idea that educationalists need not shoulder a share of the blame for the 'failure' of working-class pupils because some working-class pupils are culturally predisposed towards unskilled positions in the labour market through which they can confirm their positions as fully-fledged members of the working class. This approach is misleading and does a disservice to the majority of young people from working class families who want to enter skilled and rewarding jobs and are willing to embark on the appropriate routes to meet these ends so long as they feel they have a reasonable chance of succeeding. The problem is that no-one is able to offer them a sense of direction or convince them that they are likely to succeed. Young people's aspirations for skilled jobs need to be developed and strategies need devising which will help them achieve these ends. Existing approaches have failed: schemes have done little to enhance the potential of those who leave school with few qualifications and vocational education in schools tends to be treated as second rate. Two-tier approaches to education and training will do little to reduce 'wastage' of talent as such a system invites discrimination. A new approach to education and training should aim to replace SCEs and GCSEs with a general leaving diploma, awarded to all pupils who have managed to attain set levels of competency in subject areas chosen by pupils on a cafeteria basis.

Changes of this nature would give young people a greater incentive to remain within the educational system which in turn may lead to the development of a more highly skilled labour force. Yet educational reform will not necessarily bring about a more equal society. Despite great efforts by American education-alists to remove the obstacles to equality of opportunity for work-ing-class and black school children, levels of social mobility in British and North American societies are comparable (Kerckhoff, 1990). In fact Kerckhoff has suggested that the two societies 'use different mechanisms to produce the same outcomes'.

While previous writers have depicted the transition from school to work as a structured and predictable process, many of them have failed to appreciate the normality of stress and have not realised that prior socialisation is rarely strong enough to make the transition an easy process. Even when the course of events follows a predictable, objective pattern and even in cases where a transition is to a life-phase or situation which is regarded as desirable, a transition can be difficult because change can be un-settling. Marriage, for example, is a highly predictable life phase: we know the probable age at which people from different social classes are likely to marry, that women tend to marry at a younger age than men, and that people tend to marry within their own social class. Prospective partners often have a good idea about what marriage entails: they will have observed marital relation-ships in the home or neighbourhood, and will have been presented with images of marriage on television and in films through-out childhood and adolescence. Yet this knowledge, the strength of prior socialisation and the subjective experience of 'free choice', is insufficient to remove the likely stress on becoming married.

Married partners must adjust to a whole new reality and way of life: they must become reconciled to new restrictions or fight against them, and at an early stage in the marriage will test and negotiate the bounds of behaviour within this new situation.

This analogy is appropriate to the process of job entry – even when job entry confirms earlier expectations and when the young person is lucky enough to avoid the experience of unemployment or the uncertainty of schemes. New workers have to adjust their expectations and behaviour in order to fit into the work situation. Employers are all too aware of the difficulties some young people encounter in adjusting to working life and may have preferences for older workers as a result of anticipated difficulties (Ashton and Field, 1976).

Youth is a difficult time in both social and psychological terms and young people making the transition to subordinate positions within the labour market do not tend to embrace their subordination as some sociologists have implied. Many young people leave school hoping to enter skilled and intrinsically rewarding jobs, but eventually become committed to unskilled work through their experiences in the labour market.

Although the 'lads' in Willis's (1977) study were a minority among their working-class peers, it is wrong to depict working-class youths as active participants in their own 'self damnation'. Tanner (1991), for example, has suggested that it is more accurate to regard Canadian high school drop-outs as 'rejected' rather than 'rejectors'. Willis's 'lads' were brought up within a strong working-class culture in a traditional manufacturing area. The rapid decline of these traditional working-class areas and cultures over the last few decades means that his analysis is dated. Indeed, Brown (1987b) found that very few young people fitted Willis's stereotype. Changes in the labour market mean that unqualified male school-leavers are more likely to find themselves wearing a theme uniform in a fast food outlet than proving their masculinity on a building site.

In many respects, the shortcoming in the theoretical explanations of the transition from school to work has been caused by sociologists' tendency to concentrate *either* on objective elements of social processes *or* on subjective aspects of human behaviour without attempting to reconcile these two dimensions of social life. In particular, the predictability of a process in objective terms *cannot* be taken to mean that socialisation will 'take care of' subjective dimensions of behaviour. Subjective interpretation is not simply a reflection of objective reality, and it is necessary to incorporate an understanding of the ways social actors make sense of the world around them and react to it. As C. Wright Mills advised us, the challenge of sociology is to understand both the objective and the subjective aspects of social life, locating them historically and interpreting the relationship between these inter-related dimensions: this is also the challenge facing researchers who are interested the transition from school to work.

Appendix I
THE DATA

AI. 1 The Scottish Young People's Surveys

The Scottish Young People's Surveys are regular postal surveys which have been carried out at the Centre for Educational Sociology, University of Edinburgh since 1977. They are multi-purpose surveys and have been funded by the Scottish Education Department, the Industry Department for Scotland, the Training Agency and the Department of Employment.

The sampling frame for the survey is provided by the Scottish Education Department who require all Scottish schools to complete a form giving details of pupils with selected birthdates. The Scottish Education Department and the Scottish Examination Board also provide population figures by gender and level of examination attainment which is used for weighting purposes. Weighting procedures are employed in order to compensate for differential rates of non-response.

The current design of the survey comprises two overlapping 'arms'; a leaver's survey and a cohort survey. Leavers' surveys have been conducted biennially since 1977, and at the time of writing dispatch of the 1991 survey is being prepared. The leavers' survey is targeted at young people who leave school in any one calendar year and includes those leaving from the third, fourth, fifth and sixth years. Questionnaires are dispatched to young people's home addresses during the spring following school-leaving (the 1977 survey, for example, covers those who had left school from the 1975/6 academic year). Those who have not responded within two weeks are sent a variety of reminders, usually including two postcard reminders and a re-administration of the questionnaire. (For details of attrition reduction methods used in the Scottish Young People's Surveys, see Dodds *et al.*, 1989.)

While separate conceptually, the cohort element overlaps the leavers' survey in that the sample comprised young people who were in the fourth year of secondary schooling in the previous academic year. This element was first introduced in 1985 (following a pilot in 1984) because leavers' surveys were not able to provide sufficient information on minimum-age school-leavers who had often not entered employment by the spring after school-leaving owing to the increasing protraction of the transition from school.

AI. 2 Leavers' surveys

The size of sample frame used for the leavers' surveys since 1977 have varied; recent surveys have used a nationally representative 10 per cent sample, but in 1977 a 40 per cent fraction was used and in 1981 a 37 per cent fraction. In addition, in 1977 the sample was confined to four selected regions: Strathclyde; Lothian; Fife, and Tayside (about three-quarters of the population of Scotland live in these four regions). Response rates have tended to be in the region of 80 per cent, although rates are higher for qualified than non-qualified school-leavers. (Full details of samples and response rates for leavers' surveys between 1977 and 1987 have been described elsewhere (Tomes, 1989b).) The data I have used from the leavers' surveys has been drawn from a specially constructed 'trends' dataset which contains 10 per cent of school-leavers in the years 1979, 1981, 1983, 1985 and 1987. The 1977 data set contains 10 per cent of school-leavers in the four selected regions.

AI. 3 The Cohort Surveys

Most of the data in this book is drawn from the 1985 cohort of the Scottish Young People's Survey. This was a 10 per cent sample of young people who had entered the fourth year of secondary schooling in autumn 1983. Members of the sample were first contacted in spring 1985 (when their average age was 16·75). They were contacted again in spring 1986 (average age 17·75), and for a third time in autumn 1987 (average age 19·25). The target sample for the cohort was 8,044 and the overall response rate to each survey sweep was in the region of 80 per cent. Approximately 50 per cent of the original sample responded to all three sweeps (4,013 sample members). Full details of response rates and samples for each sweep have been provided elsewhere (Furlong and Raffe, 1989). In Chapter 7 information from the 1989 cohort has been used. The sample design was identical to that of the 1985 cohort: 10 per cent of young people who entered the fourth year of secondary schooling in autumn 1987. This cohort was followed-up in autumn 1991, but information in Chapter 7 refers to the first sweep only. The target sample for the 1989 cohort was 7,259, and the response rate was 80 per cent.

Appendix II

MULTIVARIATE ANALYSIS

AII. 1

This Appendix provides full details of the multivariate analyses used in the book, including descriptions of the variables and tables on which earlier discussions were based.

AII. 2

The logit model discussed in Chapter 3 predicts the relative chances of minimum-age school-leavers having entered a 'respectable' job in comparison to a young person from the professional and managerial class who left school with five or more O grades in 1977. This model is presented in Table A. 1 with outcomes displayed as coefficients and exponentiated to show relative chances. Independent variables are included to describe father's social class, total SCE qualifications on leaving school and year in which the young person left school.

AII. 3

The second logit model in chapter 3 (Table A. 2) predicts the relative chances of unemployment in autumn 1987 among minimum-age school-leavers in comparison to a young person from the professional and managerial class with five or more O grades who left school in 1979. The same independent variables are used as in the previous model.

AII. 4

The first multivariate model in chapter 5 predicts total unemployment in weeks up to autumn 1987 among young people who had entered the labour market by spring 1985 (and who were still in the labour market in autumn 1987). The model was constructed separately for males and females (Tables A. 3a and A. 3b).

A range of dummy variables was used to describe, respectively: young people with different SCE attainments from school (omitted category no awards/DE grades); those who reported obtaining vocational qualifications other than Scotvec Modules (such as Scottec or Scotbec certificates or diplomas, CGLI, RSA or equivalent) since school; and those who left school at Christmas of S5 (the others had left from S4). The number of Scotvec modules completed was included as an interval scale variable. Dummy variables were also included to describe those who had experience of YTS and those whose fathers were unemployed in autumn 1987. Father's occupational status in spring 1985 as measured on the Cambridge Occupational Status Scale was included as an interval scale variable.

In order to describe the local labour market, I used information from the Scottish Young People's Surveys on the proportion of minimum-age school-leavers within a travel-to-work-area, and the proportion of young people who experienced YTS in each travel-to-work-area. The occupational structure of the area was described using information from the 1981 Census on the proportion of workers in BROADWOC categories 1-3, 4, 5, 6 (omitted category 6). The industrial structure of the area was described by information from the 1984 Census of Employment and this describes the proportion of workers in agricultural and service sector industries (SIC 0 and 6 to 9). The all-age unemployment rate in October 1987 within the travel-to-work-area within which the respondent's school was located, was also included as an interval scale variable.

AII. 5

The second multivariate model in Chapter 5 is a logit model which is used to predict the relative chances of unemployment in autumn 1987 among minimum-age school-leavers with a range of post-school experiences (Table A. 4). Dummy variables were used to describe school-leavers who were aged 18 or over in April 1986 and who had a father who was unemployed in October 1987. School qualifications were also described by a series of dummy variables (the omitted category being those with who did not sit SCE examinations), as was father's social class (the omitted category being semi- and unskilled manual workers). Labour market experience is described by a set of dummy variables indicating stage of leaving school (omitted category being after S4), and whether the young person was unemployed in the autumn or spring after leaving school (autumn for S4 leavers, spring for Christmas leavers). Unemployment in the local labour market is described by a co-variate measuring all-age unemployment in the travel-to-work-area in October 1987. Finally, YTS experience is measured by a series of dummies describing whether respondents had ever experienced YTS, whether they had ever completed a YTS scheme and whether they were unemployed immediately after leaving YTS.

AII. 6

The multivariate model in Chapter 7 is a multiple regression model which is used to predict occupational aspirations among the 1987 Scottish Young People's Survey cohort (Table A. 5). Occupational aspirations were collapsed into three categories for the purposes of this analysis: professional, managerial and related careers; clerical and skilled manual and service occupations; and operatives, labourers and other unskilled occupations. Dummy variables were included to describe: SCE qualifications gained by the end of fourth year (omitted category being no O grade passes); whether the young person was still in full-time education; father's social class (omitted category being lower working class); current occupation (omitted category being semi- and unskilled occupations); and whether a young person had experienced YTS.

AII.7

The first multivariate model described in Chapter 8 is a logit model predicting employment in autumn 1987 among young people who were in the labour market in autumn 1987 and who had entered the labour market by spring 1985 (Table A. 6). The independent variables in this model are the same as those described for Tables A. 3a and A.3b.

AII.8

The second multivariate model described in Chapter 8 is a multiple regression model predicting the Cambridge occupational status scores of young people who were in full-time jobs in autumn 1987 and who had entered the labour market by spring 1985. The model is presented separately for males and females (Tables A.7a and A.7b). The independent variables in this model are also the same as those described for Tables A. 3a and A.3.b.

TABLE A. 1 Logit model predicting relative chances of minimum-age school-leavers having entered a 'respectable' job*

	Male Relative Chances	GLIM Coefficient	(SE)	Female Relative Chances	GLIM Coefficient	(SE)
Upper Working Class	1.3	0.2663	(0.08)	0.7	-0.3146	(0.10)
Lower Working Class	0.9	-0.1170	(0.09)	0.6	-0.5519	(0.11)
3-4 0 Grades	0.8	-0.1924	(0.15)	0.9	-0.1449	(0.17)
1-2 0 Grades	0.5	-0.6756	(0.13)	0.4	-1.037	(0.16)
No Award/DE	0.2	-1.438	(0.12)	0.2	-1.678	(0.15)
1979	0.9	-0.06473	(0.09)	0.9	-0.1015	(0.10)
1981	0.7	-0.3565	(0.10)	0.5	-0.7353	(0.11)
1983	0.8	-0.2424	(0.10)	0.4	-0.9874	(0.12)
1985	0.6	-0.4535	(0.12)	0.3	-1.099	(0.13)
1987	0.6	-0.4630	(0.11)	0.4	-1.021	(0.12)

Note: *Compared to professional and managerial class with 5 or more O grades in 1977.

TABLE A.2 Logit model predicting relative chances of minimum-age school-leavers being continuously unemployed up to the spring after leaving school*

	Male Relative Chances	GLIM Coefficient	(SE)	Female Relative Chances	GLIM Coefficient	(SE)
Upper WorkingClass	0.9	-0.1418	(0.19)	0.9	-0.06954	(0.20)
Lower Working Class	1.1	0.1318	(0.20)	1.0	0.03092	(0.22)
3-4 0 Grades	0.9	-0.1391	(0.43)	0.6	-0.4575	(0.40)
1-2 0 Grades	1.5	0.3957	(0.35)	1.1	0.07052	(0.33)
No Award/DE	2.8	1.033	(0.33)	2.0	0.6952	(0.30)
1981	0.7	-0.3308	(0.22)	1.3	0.2525	(0.21)
1983	1.3	0.2667	(0.19)	1.6	0.4681	(0.20)
1985	1.6	0.5015	(0.19)	1.9	0.6636	(0.20)
1987	1.8	0.5798	(0.20)	2.5	0.9186	(0.21)

Note: *Compared to professional and managerial class with 5 or more O grades in 1979.

TABLE A.3a Multiple regression predicting total unemployment (weeks) up to autumn 1987 among young people who had entered the labour market by spring 1985, and were in the labour market in autumn 1987 – male

	(a) b	(a) t	(b) b	(b) t	(c) b	(c) t	(d) b	(d) t	(e) b	(e) t	(f) b	(f) t	(g) b	(g) t
1-2 O Grades	-25.401	(6.7)	-22.534	(6.0)	-21.755	(5.8)	-21.570	(5.8)	-21.440	(5.8)	-21.320	(5.7)	-22.146	(6.0)
3-4 O Grades	-32.413	(6.9)	-26.065	(5.6)	-24.700	(5.2)	-23.979	(5.1)	-24.173	(5.2)	-23.892	(5.1)	-25.671	(5.9)
5+ O Grades	-37.183	(6.4)	-26.978	(4.5)	-25.824	(4.3)	-24.920	(4.2)	-24.575	(4.1)	-24.942	(4.2)	-26.410	(4.5)
Modules			-0.570	(2.5)	-0.546	(2.4)	-0.495	(2.2)	-0.485	(2.2)	-0.477	(2.1)	-0.485	(2.2)
Voc. Qual.			-22.697	(4.8)	-22.615	(4.8)	-22.374	(4.9)	-22.685	(4.9)	-23.262	(5.0)	-22.635	(4.9)
Xmas	-5.848	(1.6)	-6.844	(1.9)	-6.649	(1.8)	-6.967	(4.2)	-6.726	(1.8)	-7.083	(1.9)	-6.659	(1.8)
YTS Ever	7.694	(2.3)	8.553	(2.6)	8.408	(2.6)	5.973	(1.8)	5.462	(1.6)	3.888	(1.1)		
Father Unemp.					11.272	(2.2)	10.345	(2.0)	9.628	(1.9)	9.332	(1.8)		
Father Camb. Score					-0.134	(1.3)	-0.106	(1.0)	0.101	(1.0)	-0.102	(1.0)		
Local Unemp.- Oct.'87							1.408	(3.6)	1.485	(2.3)	0.743	(1.0)	1.697	(2.6)
Min. Age Leavers in TTWA (male)											-0.313	(1.7)		
Experience of YTS inTTWA (male)											0.373	(2.1)		
Total Emp. in BROADWOC1-3 inTTWA (male)									61.685	(1.0)	70.117	(1.1)	60.146	(0.9)
Total Emp. in BROADWOC4 inTTWA (male)									106.869	(1.1)	22.618	(0.2)	130.576	(1.3)
Total Emp. in BROADWOC5 inTTWA(male)									91.511	(1.1)	84.659	(1.0)	94.283	(1.1)
Total Emp.in Service Industries inTTWA (male)									4.048	(0.2)	2.768	(0.1)		
R2	.111		.149		.156		.169		.175		.181		.168	
Constant	46.834	(14.4)	49.056	(15.3)	50.602	(12.2)	29.790	(4.2)	-23.971	(0.8)	-2.980	(0.1)	27.088	(0.9)

Notes: WOC1–WOC5 = managerial & administrative, higher level service and industrial occupations. WOC4 = lower level

Table A.5 Multiple regression predicting total unemployment (weeks) up to autumn 1987 among young people who had entered the labour market by spring 1985, and were in the labour market in autumn 1987 – female

	(a) b	(a) t	(b) b	(b) t	(c) b	(c) t	(d) b	(d) t	(e) b	(e) t	(f) b	(f) t	(g) b	(g) t
1-2 O Grades	-21.435	(4.7)	-20.985	(4.6)	-19.152	(4.2)	-18.756	(4.1)	-19.448	(4.2)	-19.615	(4.3)	-20.736	(4.6)
3-4 O Grades	-23.299	(4.5)	-22.427	(4.4)	-20.276	(3.9)	-19.935	(3.9)	-20.418	(3.9)	-20.418	(3.9)	-22.052	(4.3)
5+ O Grades	-33.410	(5.8)	-30.981	(5.3)	-27.133	(4.5)	-27.095	(4.5)	-27.594	(4.6)	-27.598	(4.6)	-30.856	(5.3)
Modules			-0.410	(0.9)	-0.340	(0.7	-0.339	(0.7)	-0.236	(0.5)	-0.219	(0.5)	-0.271	(0.6)
Voc. Qual.			-16.188	(1.7)	-15.329	(1.6)	-16.329	(1.7)	-17.706	(1.9)	-17.293	(1.9)	-18.849	(2.0)
Xmas	-1.006	(0.2)	-1.402	(0.3)	-1.527	(0.4)	-2.045	(0.5)	-2.456	(0.6)	-2.651	(0.6)	-2.505	(0.6)
YTS Ever	1.659	(0.4)	2.304	(0.3)	1.580	(0.4)	-0.167	(0.4)	1.110	(0.3)	0.629	(0.1)		
Father Unemp.					12.071	(2.1)	10.756	(1.9)	11.217	(2.0)	11.110	(1.9)		
Father Camb. Score							-0.237	(1.9)	-0.215	(1.7)	-0.222	(1.7)		
Local Unemp. – Oct.'87					-0.272	(2.2)	0.809	(1.6)	1.077	(1.7)	0.929	(1.3)	1.462	(2.4)
Min. Age Leavers inTTWA(female)											0.071	(0.3)		
Experience of YTS in TTWA (female)											0.116	(0.6)		
Total Emp. in BROADWOCl–3 in TTWA (female)									-24.355	(0.9)	-22.053	(0.8)	-20.834	(0.8)
Total Emp. in BROADWOC4 in TTWA (female)									19.420	(1.2)	19.586	(1.3)	18.427	(1.2)
Total Emp. in BROADWOC5 in TTWA (female)									96.026	(0.2)	63.128	(0.2)	78.594	(0.2)
Total Emp. in Service Industries inTTWA(female)									57.087	(2.1)	64.376	(2.1)	57.818	(2.1)
R2	.076		.082		.098		.102		.116		.117		.105	
Constant	45.010	(11.4)	45.438	(11.5)	49.661	(10.1)	37.983	(4.4)	-12.951	(0.5)	-22.840	(0.7)	-21.602	(0.8)

Notes: WOCl–WOC3 = managerial & administrative, higher level service and industrial occupations. WOC4 = lower level service and supervisory occupations. WOC5 = craft & skilled manual occupations and foremen.

TABLE A.4 Logit model predicting relative chances of
unemployment† in 1987

	Males			Females		
	Relative Chances	Coeff.	SE	Relative Chances	Coeff.	SE
Age 18	0.9	-0.1563	0.08	0.9	-0.1475	0.08
Unemployed father	1.6*	0.4672	0.08	1.5*	0.4163	0.08
Father in prof./ managerial occup.	1.0	0.007242	0.11	1.0	0.04803	0.12
Father in skilled occup.	0.8	-0.1724	0.10	0.9	-0.07245	0.11
Father's occupation not given	1.1	0.1154	0.11	1.0	-0.04496	0.11
4+ O Grades	0.8	-0.1778	0.11	0.9	-0.97842	0.11
1–3 O Grades	0.7*	-0.3768	0.10	0.8	0.04803	
Fails at O Grade	1.0	0.01388	0.10	0.9	-0.07245	0.11
Local unemp. rate	1.1 *	0.07239	0.02	1.0	0.03272	0.02
Christmas leaver	1.0	0.01655	0.08	1.1	0.1223	0.08
Unemployed after leaving school	1.9*	0.6228	0.08	1.6*	0.4487	0.08
Ever on YTS	0.8*	-0.2112	0.08	0.8*	-0.1744	0.08
Completed YTS	1.1	0.09726	0.08	1.2*	0.1844	0.08
Unemployed immed. after YTS	1.6*	0.4524	0.08	1.7*	0.5372	0.08

Notes: Predictors significant at the 5 per cent level are marked with an
asterisk.
† includes respondents on unemployment-based schemes such as
CP & JTS.

TABLE A.5 Multiple regression predicting occupational
aspirations among the 1987 cohort

	Males		Females	
	b	t	b	t
1–4 0 Grades	0.0290	(0.6)	0.1242	(3.3)*
5+ 0 Grades	0.4230	(8.6)*	0.5426	(12.8)*
In full-time education	0.5001	(9.9)*	0.0741	(1.6)
Upper working class	-0.0058	(0.1)	0.0330	(1.0)
Professional and managerial class	0.1569	(3.8)*	0.1264	(3.7)*
Current job – clerical or skilled	0.0145	(2.7)	0.0341	(1.2)
Current job – professional or managerial	0.5085	(3.0)*	0.3463	(2.4)*
Experience of YTS	0.0730	(1.6)	-0.2182	(4.6)*
R_2	0.2945		0.2292	
Constant	1.7344	(34.4)	2.0608	(42.1)

Note: Predictors significant at the 5 per cent level are marked with an
asterisk.

TABLE A.6 Logit model predicting employment in autumn 1987 among young people who were in the labour market in autumn 1987 and had entered the labour market by spring 1985

	Males Relative Chances	Coeff.	SE	Females Relative Chances	Coeff.	SE
1-2 O Grades	1.091	0.27	3.0*	0.3762	0.29	1.4
3–4 O Grades	1.231	0.42	3.4*	0.7027	0.33	2.0*
5+ O Grades	0.9325	0.52	2.5	0.7790	0.45	2.2
Modules	0.05346	0.06	1.0	0.1250	0.11	1.1
Voc. Qual.	1.001	0.37	2.7*	0.05234	0.46	1.0
Xmas	-0.1795	0.21	0.8	-0.4455	0.24	0.6
YTS Ever	-1.054	0.50	0.3*	-0.3229	0.43	0.7
Father Unemp.	-0.7937	0.29	0.4*	-0.6380	0.34	0.5
Father Camb. Score	0.009698	0.04	1.0	0.02128	0.03	1.0
Local Unemp. – Oct. 1987	-0.3820	0.23	0.7	-0.1113	0.15	0.9
Min. Age Leavers	-0.1666	0.07	0.8*	0.02159	0.04	1.0
Experience of YTS inTTWA	0.09177	0.04	1.1*	0.04949	0.04	1.0
Total Emp. in BROADWOC 1–3 inTTWA	-5.448	12.68	0.0	3.484	3.20	32.6
Total Emp. in BROADWOC4 in TTWA	2.029	1.63	7.6	-0.1602	0.28	0.8
Total Emp. in BROADWOC 5 in TTWA	2.247	1.30	9.4	2.344	6.28	10.4
Total Emp. in Service Industries in TTWA	-3.244	8.10	0.0	4.016	5.88	55.5

TABLE A.7a Multiple regression predicting Cambridge status scores of young people in full-time jobs in autumn 1987 who had entered the labour market by spring 1985 – male

	(a) b	(a) t	(b) b	(b) t	(c) b	(c) t	(d) b	(d) t	(e) b	(e) t	(f) b	(f) t	(g) b	(g) t
1-2 O Grades	2.222	(2.5)	2.251	(2.5)	2.233	(2.5)	2.232	(2.5)	2.218	(2.5)	2.203	(2.5)	2.226	(2.5)
3-4 O Grades	4.374	(4.2)	4.525	(4.2)	4.430	(4.1)	4.430	(4.1)	4.340	(4.0)	4.357	(4.0)	4.495	(4.2)
5+ O Grades	7.336	(5.9)	7.617	(5.9)	7.542	(5.9)	7.537	(5.9)	7.578	(5.9)	7.570	(5.8)	7.730	(6.0)
Modules			0.008	(0.2)	0.004	(0.1)	0.004	(0.1)	0.005	(0.1)	0.001	(0.2)	0.007	(0.1)
Voc. Qual.			-1.044	(1.1)	-1.009	(1.0)	-1.010	(1.0)	-1.070	(1.1)	-0.947	(0.9)	-1.135	(1.1)
Xmas	0.406	(0.5)	0.279	(0.3)	0.284	(0.3)	0.287	(0.3)	0.349	(0.4)	0.387	(0.4)	0.314	(0.3)
YTS Ever	-0.437	(0.6)	-0.390	(0.5)	-0.388	(0.5)	-0.368	(0.5)	-0.492	(0.6)	-0.240	(0.3)		
Father Unemp.					-1.593	(1.2)	-1.581	(1.2)	-1.760	(1.3)	-1.665	(1.2)		
Father Camb. Score					0.015	(0.6)	0.014	(0.6)	0.014	(0.6)	0.014	(0.6)		
Local Unemp. – Oct.'87							-0.011	(0.1)	0.057	(0.4)	0.131	(0.8)	0.030	(0.2)
Min Age Leavers in TTWA (male)											0.011	(0.3)		
Experience of YTS in TTWA (male)											-0.060	(1.5)		
Total Emp in BROADWOC1-3 in TTWA (male)									10.058	(0.7)	4.800	(0.3)	9.406	(0.6)
Total Emp in BROADWOC 4 in TTWA (male)									1.294	(0.8)	1.838	(1.1)	1.151	(0.7)
Total Emp in BROADWOC5 inTTWA(male)									0.312	(0.2)	0.222	(0.2)	0.271	(0.2)
Total Emp in Service Industries inTTWA (male)									0.094	(0.0)	-0.762	(0.1)	0.167	(0.0)
R2	.076		.078		.081		.081		.086		.090		.082	
Constant	22.772	(35.3)	27.876	(35.1)	27.661	(26.8)	27.831	(16.7)	21.231	(3.0)	23.297	(2.6)	21.995	(3.2)

Notes: WOC1–WOC3 = managerial & administrative, higher level service and industrial occupations. WOC4 = lower level service and supervisory occupations. WOC5 = craft & skilled manual occupations and foremen.

TABLE A.7b Multiple regression predicting Cambridge status scores of young people in full-time jobs in autumn 1987 who had entered the labour market by spring 1985 – female

	(a)		(b)		(c)		(d)		(e)		(f)		(g)	
	b	t	b	t	b	t	b	t	b	t	b	t	b	t
1-2 O Grades	5.175	(3.9)	5.046	(3.8)	4.514	(3.4)	4.196	(3.2)	3.691	(2.9)	3.628	(2.8)	4.001	(3.1)
3-4 O Grades	8.821	(6.1)	8.530	(5.9)	8.130	(5.7)	7.872	(5.6)	7.433	(5.3)	7.426	(5.3)	7.454	(5.4)
5+ O Grades	13.247	(8.4)	12.534	(7.8)	11.706	(7.1)	11.821	(7.3)	11.594	(7.3)	11.645	(7.3)	11.698	(7.6)
Modules			0.218	(1.8)	0.199	(1.6)	0.187	(1.5)	0.208	(1.7)	0.214	(1.8)	0.244	(2.1)
Voc. Qual.	0.024	(0.0)	2.319	(0.9)	1.905	(0.8)	2.644	(1.1)	2.864	(1.2)	2.840	(1.2)	3.258	(1.4)
Xmas	-0.258	(0.2)	0.180	(0.1)	0.209	(0.2)	0.501	(0.4)	0.502	(0.4)	0.524	(0.4)	0.678	(0.5)
YTS Ever			-0.557	(0.5)	-0.348	(0.3)	0.894	(0.8)	1.899	(1.7)	1.686	(1.4)		
Father Unemp.					0.187	(0.1)	1.202	(0.7)	1.195	(0.7)	1.151	(0.7)		
Father Camb. Score					0.093	(2.7)	0.071	(2.1)	0.067	(2.0)	0.064	(1.9)		
Local Unemp.- Oct.'87							-0.526	(4.0)	-0.454	(2.7)	-0.518	(2.7)	-0.443	(2.7)
Min. Age Leavers in TTWA (female)											0.008	(0.1)		
Experience of YTS in TTWA (female)											0.045	(0.8)		
Total Emp. in BROADWOC1-3 in TTWA (female)									-4.561	(1.6)	-4.375	(1.5)	-4.574	(1.6)
Total Emp. in BROADWOC4 in TTWA (female)									0.174	(0.6)	0.157	(0.5)	0.170	(0.5)
Total Emp. in BROADWOC5 in TTWA (female)									-4.707	(0.6)	-6.203	(0.7)	-2.940	(0.4)
Total Emp. in Service Industries in TTWA (female)									16.118	(2.3)	17.877	(2.3)	15.617	(2.8)
R2	.162		.171		.185		.214		.258		.259		.246	
Constant	36.358	(30.9)	36.207	(30.9)	34.020	(23.6)	41.471	(17.7)	29.424	(4.2)	27.743	(3.1)	32.176	(4.7)

Notes: WOCI–WOC3 = managerial & administrative, higher level seNice and industrial occupations. WOC4 = lower level

BIBLIOGRAPHY

Ainley, P. (1986) 'Shades of Prison House: Working Class Resistance to State Intervention in the Established Transition From School to Work', Paper presented to the BSA Annual Conference, Loughborough.

Aries, P. (1962) *Centuries of Childhood: A Social History of Family Life*, Cape, London.

Ashton, D. N. (1973) 'The Transition from School to Work: Notes on the Development of Different Frames of Reference Among Young Male Workers', *Sociological Review*, Vol. 21 (1), pp. 101-25.

Ashton, D. N. (1986) *Unemployment Under Capitalism*, Wheatsheaf, Brighton.

Ashton, D. N. (1988) 'Sources of Variation in Labour Market Segmentation: A Comparison of Youth Labour Markets in Canada and Britain', *Work, Employment and Society*, Vol. 2 (1), pp. 1-24.

Ashton, D. N. and Field, D. (1976) *Young Workers*, Hutchinson, London.

Ashton, D. N., Maguire, M. J. and Garland, V. (1982) *Youth in the Labour Market*, Research Paper No. 34, Department of Employment, London.

Ashton, D. N. and Maguire, M. J. (1983) *The Vanishing Youth Labour Market*, Youthaid, London.

Ashton, D. N., Maguire, M. J., Bowden, D., Dellow, P. Kennedy, S., Stanley, G., Woodhead, G. and Jennings, B. (1986) *Young Adults in the Labour Market*, Research Paper No. 55, Department of Employment, London.

Ashton, D. N., Maguire, M. J. and Spilsbury, M. (1988) 'Local Labour Markets and their Impact on the Life Chances of Youths', in Coles, B. (Ed.) *Young Careers: The Search For Work and the New Vocationalism*, Open University Press, Milton Keynes.

Ashton, D. N., Maguire, M. J. and Spilsbury, M. (1990) *Restructuring the Labour Market: The Implications for Youth*, Macmillan, London.

Ashton, D. N. and Sung, J. (1991) 'The Determinants of Labour Market Transitions in a Segmented Labour Market', Centre for Labour Market Studies, University of Leicester.

Bain, R. K. and Anderson, J. G. (1974) 'School Context and Peer Influence on Educational Plans of Adolescents', *Review of Educational Research*, Vol. 44 (4), pp. 429-45.

Bakke, E. W. (1933) *The Unemployed Man*, Nisbet, London.

Ball, S. J. (1981) *Beachside Comprehensive: A Case Study of Secondary Schooling*, Cambridge University Press, Cambridge.

Banks, M. H. and Ullah, P. (1988) *Youth Unemployment in the 1980s: Its Psychological Effects*, Croom Helm, Beckenham.

Bates, I. (1989) 'No Bleeding, Whining Minnies: The Role of YTS in Class and Gender Reproduction' *British Journal of Education and Work*, Vol. 3 (2), pp. 91-110.

Bedeman, T. and Harvey, J. (1981) *Young People on YOP*, Research and Development Series No. 3, MSC, Sheffield.

Bell, C., Howieson, C., King, K. and Raffe, D. (1988) *Liaisons Dangereuses? Education–Industry Relationship in the First Scottish TVEI Pilot Projects: An Evaluation Report*, The Training Agency, Sheffield.

Bernstein, B. (1971) *Class, Codes and Control, Volume 1*, Routledge and Kegan Paul, London.

Biddle, B. J. (1983) 'Youth Research Models and Social Policy', in Anderson, D. S. and Blakers, C. (Eds.) *Youth Transition and Social Research*, Australian National University Press, Canberra.

Blackman, S. (1987) 'The Labour Market in School: New Vocationalism and Issues of Socially Ascribed Discrimination', in Brown, P. and Ashton, D. N. (Eds.) *Education, Unemployment and Labour Markets*, Falmer, Lewes.

Bourdieu, P. (1973) 'Cultural Reproduction and Social Reproduction', in Brown, R. (Ed.) *Knowledge, Education and Cultural Change*, Tavistock, London.

Bourdieu, P. (1974) 'The School as a Conservative Force: Scholastic and Cultural Inequalities', in Eggleston, J. (Ed.) *Contemporary Research in the Sociology of Education*, Methuen, London.

Bowles, S. (1975) 'Unequal Education and the Reproduction of the Social Division of Labour', in Coxon, A. P. M. and Jones, C. L. (Eds.) *Social Mobility*, Penguin, Harmondsworth.

Bowles, S. and Gintis, H. (1976) *Schooling in Capitalist America: Education Reform and the Contradictions of Economic Life*, Basic Books, New York.

Braverman, H. (1974) *Labour and Monopoly Capital*, Monthly Review Press, New York.

Breen, R. (1986) 'Does Experience of Work Help School-Leavers Get a Job?', *Sociology*, Vol. 20 (2), pp. 207-27.

Brown, P. (1987a) 'The New Vocationalism: A Policy for Inequality', in Coles, B. (Ed.) *Young Careers: The Search For Jobs and the New Vocationalism*, Open University Press, Milton Keynes.

Brown, P. (1987b) *Schooling Ordinary Kids: Inequality, Unemployment and the New Vocationalism*, Tavistock, London.

Burnhill, P. (1984) 'The Ragged Edge of Compulsory Schooling', in Raffe, D. (Ed.) *Fourteen to Eighteen: The Changing Pattern of Schooling in Scotland*, Aberdeen University Press, Aberdeen.

Burnhill, P., Garner, C. and MacPherson, A. F. (1988) 'Social Change, School Attainment and Entry into Higher Education 1976 to 1986', in Raffe, D. (Ed.) *Education and the Youth Labour Market*, Falmer, London.

Bynner, J. (1991) 'Transitions to Work: Results from a Longitudinal Study of Young People in Four British Labour Markets', in Ashton, D. N. and Lowe, G. (Eds.) *Making their Way: Education, Training and the Labour Market in Canada and Britain*, Open University Press, Milton Keynes.

Carter, M. P. (1962) *Home, School and Work*, Pergamon Press, London.

Clarke, J. and Critcher, C. (1985) *The Devil Makes Work: Leisure in Capitalist*

Britain, Macmillan, London.

Clough, E., Gray, J., Jones, B. and Pattie, C. (1986) *Routes Through YTS*, Research and Development No. 42, Youth Cohort Studies No. 2, Manpower Services Commission, Sheffield.

Cockburn, C. (1987) *Two Track Training: Sex Inequalities and the YTS*, Macmillan, Basingstoke.

Coffield, F., Borrill, C. and Marshall, S. (1983) 'How Young People Try to Survive Being Unemployed', *New Society*, 2nd June, pp. 332-3.

Coffield, F, Borrill, C., and Marshall, S. (1986) *Growing Up at the Margins*, Open University Press, Milton Keynes.

Cohen, P. (1982) 'School for Dole', *New Socialist*, January/February, pp. 43-7.

Coles, B. (1986) 'School-Leaver, Job-Seeker, Dole-Reaper: Young and Unemployed in Rural England', in Allen, S., Waton, A., Purcell, K. and Wood, S. (Eds.) *The Experience of Unemployment*, Macmillan, London.

Delamont, S. (1980) *Sex Roles and the School*, Methuen, London.

Department of Education and Science, (1973) *Careers Education in Secondary School*, HMSO, London.

Dodds, S., Furlong, A. and Croxford, L. (1989) 'Quality and Quantity: Tackling Non-Contact Attrition in a Longitudinal Survey', *Sociology*, Vol. 23 (2), pp. 275-84.

Douglas, J. W. B. (1967) *The Home and the School*, Panther, St. Albans.

Douvan, A. and Adelson, J. (1966) The Adolescent Experience, Wiley, New York.

Eisenberg, P. and Lazarsfeld, P. F. (1938) 'The Psychological Effects of Unemployment', *Psychological Bulletin*, Vol. 35, (4), pp. 359-90.

Erikson, E. H. (1968) *Identity, Youth and Crisis*, Norton, New York.

Feuer, L. S. (1969) *The Conflict of Generations: The Character and Significance of Student Movements*, Basic Books, New York.

Floud, J. E., Halsey, A. H. and Martin, F. M. (Eds.) (1957) *Social Class and Educational Opportunity*, Heinemann, London.

Ford, J. (1969) *Social Class and the Comprehensive School*, Routledge and Kegan Paul, London.

Fox, A. (1971) *A Sociology of Work and Industry*, Collier-Macmillan, London.

Fraser, D. (1973) *The Evolution of the British Welfare State*, Macmillan, London.

Freeman, D. (1983) *Margaret Mead and Samoa: The Unmaking of an Anthropological Myth*, Penguin, London.

Furlong, A. (1986) 'Schools and the Structure of Female Occupational Aspirations', *British Journal of Sociology of Education*, Vol. 7 (4), pp. 367-77.

Furlong, A. (1987) 'Coming to Terms with the Declining Demand For Youth Labour', in Brown, P. and Ashton, D. N. (Eds.) *Education, Unemployment and Labour Markets*, Falmer, Lewes.

Furlong, A. (1988a) 'The Effects of Youth Unemployment on the Transition From School', Ph. D Thesis, University of Leicester.

Furlong, A. (1988b) '... But They Don't Want To Work, Do They? Unemployment and Work Ethics Among Young People in Scotland' in

Raffe, D. (Ed.) *Education and the Youth Labour Market*, Falmer, Basingstoke.

Furlong, A. (1990a) 'A Decade of Decline: Social Class and Post-School Destinations of Minimum-Age School-Leavers', in Wallace, C. and Cross, M. (Eds.) *Youth in Transition: The Sociology of Youth and Youth Policy*, Falmer, Basingstoke.

Furlong, A. (1990b) 'Labour Market Segmentation and the Age Structuring of Employment Opportunities for Young People', *Work, Employment and Society*, Vol. 4 (2). pp. 253-69.

Furlong, A. (1991) 'Differences Within Scotland in Young People's Routes into the Labour Market', in Furlong, A., Main, B. and Raffe, D. *Young People's Routes into and Within the Labour Market*, Industry Department for Scotland, Edinburgh.

Furlong, A. and Raffe, D. (1989) *Young People's Routes into the Labour Market*, ESU Research Paper No. 17, Industry Department for Scotland, Edinburgh.

Furlong, A. and Spearman, M. (1989) 'Psychological Well-Being and the Transition from School', *British Journal of Education and Work*, Vol. 3 (1), pp. 49-55.

Furlong, A., Campbell, R. and Roberts, K. (1990) 'The Effects of Post-16 Experiences and Social Class on the Leisure Patterns of Young Adults', *Leisure Studies*, Vol. 9 (1), pp. 213-24.

Furlong, A. and Cooney, G. H. (1990) 'Getting on their Bikes: Teenagers Leaving Home in Scotland in the 1980s', *Journal of Social Policy*, Vol. 19 (4), pp. 535-51.

Garner, C. (1989) *Does Deprivation Damage?*, Report to the John Watson's Trust, Edinburgh.

Garner, C., Main, B. G. M. and Raffe, D. (1988) 'A Tale of Four Cities: Social and Spatial Inequalities in the Youth Labour Market', in Raffe, D. (Ed.) *Education and the Youth Labour Market*, Falmer, Lewes.

Gillis, J. R. (1981) *Youth and History: Tradition and Change in European Age Relations, 1770–Present*, Academic Press, New York.

Ginzberg, E., Ginsburg, S. W., Axelrad, S. and Herma, J. L. (1951) *Occupational Choice*, Columbia University Press, New York.

Goffman, E. (1952) 'On Cooling the Mark Out', *Psychiatry*, Vol. 15 (4), pp. 451-63.

Goldberg, D. (1972) *The Detection of Psychiatric Illness by Questionnaire*, Oxford University Press, London.

Goldthorpe, J., Lockwood, D., Bechhofer, F. and Platt, J. (1968) *The Affluent Worker: Industrial Attitudes and Behaviour*, Cambridge University Press, Cambridge.

Goldthorpe, J., Lockwood, D., Bechhofer, F. and Platt, J. (1969) *The Affluent Worker in the Class Structure*, Cambridge University Press, Cambridge.

Gramsci, A. (1971) *Selections from the Prison Notebooks*, Lawrence and Wishart, London.

Gray, J., McPherson, A. F. and Raffe, D. (1983) *Reconstructions of Secondary Education: Theory, Myth and Practice Since the War*, Routledge and Kegan Paul, London.

Griffin, C. (1985) *Typical Girls*, Routledge and Kegan Paul, London.

Griffin, C. (1986) 'Broken Transition: From School to the Scrapheap' paper presented to the British Sociological Association Annual Conference, Loughborough.

Hakim, C. (1979) *Occupational Segregation: A Comparative Study of the Degree and Pattern of the Differentiation Between Men's and Women's Work in Britain, the United States and Other Countries*, Department of Employment, London.

Hall, G. Stanley (1904) *Adolescence: Its Psychology and Its Relations to Physiology, Anthropology, Sociology, Sex, Crime, Religion and Education*, 2 Vols., Appleton, New York.

Hall, S. and Jefferson, T. (1976) (Eds.) *Resistance Through Rituals: Youth Subcultures in Post-War Britain*, Hutchinson, London.

Halsey, A. H., Heath, A. F. and Ridge, J. M. (1980) *Origins and Destinations*, Clarendon Press, Oxford.

Hargreaves, D. (1967) *Social Relations in a Secondary School*, Routledge and Kegan Paul, London.

Harris, C. C. (1987) *Redundancy and Recession in South Wales*, Blackwell, Oxford.

Hayes, J. (1970) 'The Home and the School in the Process of Vocational Development', *Careers Quarterly*, Vol. 22 (2), pp. 28-31.

Hayes, J. and Nutman, P. (1981) *Understanding the Unemployed*, Tavistock, London.

Heath, A. (1981) *Social Mobility*, Fontana, London.

Hendry, L. B., Raymond, M. and Stewart, C. (1984) 'Unemployment, School and Leisure: An Adolescent Study', *Leisure Studies*, Vol. 3, pp. 175-87.

Hill, J. (1978) 'The psychological Impact of Unemployment', *New Society*, 19 January, pp. 118-20.

Hockley, J. (1984) *The Implementation of the Youth Training Scheme in Three Local Labour Markets*, Report to the Department of Employment, London.

Holland, G. (1977) *Young People and Work*, MSC, Sheffield.

Hopson, B. and Hayes, J. (1972) *The Theory and Practice of Vocational Guidance*, Pergamon Press, Oxford.

Hopson, B. and Adams, J. (1976) 'Towards an Understanding of Transition: Defining Some Boundaries of Transition Dynamics', in Hopson, B. and Adams, J. (Eds.) *Transition*, Martin Robertson, London.

Hoskins, M., Sung, J. and Ashton, D. N. (1989) 'Job Competition and the Entry to Work', Discussion Paper No. 111, Department of Economics, University of Leicester.

Hutson, S. and Jenkins, R. (1987) 'Growing Up in South Wales', in Brown, P. and Ashton. D. N. (Eds.) *Education and the Youth Labour Market*, Falmer, Basingstoke.

Jackson, B. and Marsden, D. (1962) *Education and the Working Class*, Routledge and Kegan Paul, London.

Jackson, P. R., Stafford, E. M., Banks, M. H. and Warr, P. (1983) 'Unemployment and Psychological Distress in Young People: The Moderating Role of Employment Commitment', *Journal of Applied Psychology*,

Vol. 68 (3), pp. 525-35.

Jahoda, M. (1987) 'Unemployed Men at Work', in Fryer, D. and Ullah, P. (Eds.) *Unemployed People: Social and Psychological Perspectives*, Open University Press, Milton Keynes.

Jahoda, M. and Chalmers, A. D. (1963) 'School Leavers Recall of the Interview with the Youth Employment Officer', *Occupational Psychology*, Vol. 37 (2), pp. 112-21.

Jehoel-Gijsbers, G. and Groot, W. (1989) 'Unemployed Youth: A Lost Generation?', *Work, Employment and Society*, Vol. 3 (4), pp. 491-508.

Jenkins, R. (1983) *Lads, Citizens and Ordinary Kids*, Routledge and Kegan Paul, London.

Jones, G. (1987a) 'Young Workers in the Class Structure', *Work, Employment and Society*, Vol. 1 (4), pp. 487-508.

Jones, G. (1987b) 'Leaving the Parental Home: An Analysis of Early Housing Careers' *Journal of Social Policy*, Vol. 32 (2), pp. 252-58.

Jones, P. (1983) 'The Effects of Rising Unemployment on School-Leavers', *Department of Employment Gazette*, January, pp. 13-16.

Jordon, B. (1982) *Mass Unemployment and the Future of Britain*, Blackwell, Oxford.

Junanker, P. N. and Neale, A. (1987) 'Relative Wages and the Youth Labour Market', in Junanker, P. N. (Ed.) *From School To Unemployment: The Labour Market for Young People*, Macmillan, London.

Kelly, K. (1989) 'When I Grow Up I Want to Be... : A Longitudinal Study of the Development of Career Preferences', *British Journal of Guidance and Counselling*, Vol. 17 (2), pp. 179-200.

Kerckhoff, A. C. (1990) *Getting Started: Transition to Adulthood in Great Britain*, Westview Press, Boulder, San Francisco and Oxford.

Kirkby, R. and Roberts, H. (1984) 'YB on YTS? Why Not', Paper Presented to the BSA Annual Conference, Bradford.

Lee, D., Marsden, D., Rickman, P. and Duncombe, J. (1990) *Scheming for Youth: A Study of YTS in the Enterprise Culture*, Open University Press, Milton Keynes.

Leonard, D. (1980) *Sex and Generation: A Study of Courtship and Weddings*, Tavistock, London.

Lodahl, M. M. and Kejner, M. (1965) 'The Definition and Measurement of Job Involvement', *Journal of Applied Psychology*, Vol. 49, pp. 24-33.

Lowden, S. (1989) 'Three Years On: The Reaction of Young People to Scotland's Action Plan', Centre for Educational Sociology, Edinburgh.

McDonald, R. (1988) 'Schooling, Training, Working and Claiming: Youth and Unemployment in Local, Rural Labour Markets', Unpublished Ph. D. Thesis, University of York.

MacKay, D. I. and Reid, G. L. (1972) 'Redundancy, Unemployment and Manpower Policy', *Economic Journal*, Vol. 82 (2), pp. 1256-72.

McPherson, A. F. and Willms, J. D. (1987) 'Equalisation and Improvement: Some Effects of Comprehensive Reorganisation in Scotland', *Sociology*, Vol. 21 (4), pp. 509-39.

Main, B. (1990) 'The Effect of the Youth Training Scheme on Employment Probability', in Furlong, A., Main, B. and Raffe, D. (1990) *Young People's Routes into the Labour Market*: Final Report Industry Department for Scotland, Edinburgh.

Main, B. and Shelly, M. (1988) 'The Effectiveness of YTS as a Manpower Policy', Discussion Paper No. 8801, University of St. Andrews. No. 8801.

Maizels, J. (1970) *Adolescent Needs and the Transition from School to Work*, Athlone Press, London.

Makeham, P. (1980) *Youth Unemployment: An Examination of Evidence on Youth Unemployment Using National Statistics*, Department of Employment, London.

Mannheim, K. (1927) *Essays in the Sociology of Knowledge*, Routledge and Kegan Paul, London.

Manpower Services Commission (1981) *A New Training Initiative: A Consultative Document*, MSC, London.

Manwaring, T. (1984) 'The Extended Internal Labour Market', *Cambridge Journal of Economics*, Vol. 8 (2), pp. 161-87.

Manwaring, T. and Wood, S. (1984) 'Recruitment and the Recession' , in Beardsworth, A. D., Bryman, A., Ford, J., and Keil, T. (Eds.) Employers and Recruitment: Explorations in Labour Demand, *International Journal of Social Economics*, Vol. 11 (7), pp. 49-63.

Marini, M. M. and Greenberger, E. (1978) 'Sex Differences in Occupational Aspirations and Expectations', *Sociology of Work and Occupations*, Vol. 5 (2), pp. 147-78.

Marsden, D. (1987 'Youth Pay in Some OECD Countries Since 1966' in Junanker, P. N. (Ed.) *From School To Unemployment: The Labour Market for Young People*, Macmillan, London.

Martin, J. and Roberts, C. (1984) *Women and Work: A Lifetime Perspective*, HMSO, London.

Mead, M. (1928) *Coming of Age in Samoa*, Penguin, Harmondsworth.

Millar, D. C. and Form, W. H. (1951) *Industrial Sociology*, Harper, New York.

Millham, S., Bullock, R. and Howsie, K. (1978) 'Juvenile Unemployment: A Concept Due for Re-Cycling', *Journal of Adolescence*, Vol. 1, pp. 11-24.

Mills, C. W. (1968) *The Sociological Imagination*, Oxford University Press, London.

Murray, C. (1989) 'Underclass', *Sunday Times Magazine*, 5th November.

Musgrave, P. W. (1967) 'Towards a Sociological Theory of Occupational Choice', *Sociological Review*, Vol. 15 (1), pp. 33-46.

Musgrove, F. (1960) 'Decline of the Educative Family', *Universities Quarterly*, Vol. 14, pp. 377-404.

Musgrove, F. (1964) *Youth and the Social Order*, Routledge and Kegan Paul, London.

Norris, G. M. (1978) 'Unemployment, Subemployment and Personal Characteristics: a) The Inadequacies of Traditional Approaches to Unemployment b) Job Separation and Work Histories: The Alternative Approach, *Sociological Review*, Vol. 26 (2), pp. 89-108; (3), pp. 327-34.

Osterman, P. (1980) *Getting Started: The Youth Labour Market*, MIT Press, Cambridge, Mass. and London.

Pahl, R. E. (1978) 'Living Without a Job: How School-Leavers See the Future', *New Society*, 2 November, pp. 259-62.

Parkin, F. (1972) *Class Inequality and Political Order*, Granada, St. Albans.

Paul, L. (1962) *The Transition from School to Work*, Industrial Welfare Society, London.

Payne, J. (1987) 'Does Unemployment Run in Families? Some Findings From the General Household Survey', *Sociology*, Vol. 21 (2), pp. 199-214.

Pearson, G. (1983) *Hooligan: A History of Respectable Fears*, Macmillan, London.

Pilgrim Trust (1938) *Men Without Work*, Cambridge University Press, Cambridge.

Plowden Report (1967) *Children and their Primary Schools*, HMSO, London.

Prandy, K. (1990) 'The Revised Cambridge Scale of Occupations' *Sociology* Vol. 24 (2), pp. 629-55.

Raffe, D. (1983a) 'Some Recent Trends in Youth Unemployment in Scotland', *Scottish Educational Review*, Vol. 15 (1), pp. 16-27.

Raffe, D. (1983b) 'Employment Instability Among Less Qualified Young Workers', *British Journal of Guidance and Counselling*, 11 (1), pp. 21-34.

Raffe, D. (1983c) 'Education and Unemployment: Does YOP Make a Difference (and Will YTS)?', in Gleeson, D. (Ed.) *Youth Training and the Search for Work*, Routledge and Kegan Paul, London.

Raffe, D. (1984a) 'The Transition From School to Work and the Recession: Evidence From the Scottish School Leavers Surveys', *British Journal of Sociology of Education*, Vol. 5 (3), pp. 247-65.

Raffe, D. (1984b) 'YOP and the Future of YTS', in Raffe, D. (Ed.) *Fourteen to Eighteen*, Aberdeen University Press, Aberdeen.

Raffe, D. (1986a) 'Unemployment and School Motivation: The Case of Truancy', *Educational Review*, Vol. 38 (1), pp. 11-19.

Raffe, D. (1986b) 'Change and Continuity in the Youth Labour Market: A Critical Review of Structural Explanations of Youth Unemployment', in Allan, S., Purcell, K., Waton, A. and Wood, S. (Eds.) *The Experience of Unemployment*, Macmillan, London.

Raffe, D. (1987) 'The Context of the Youth Training Scheme: An Analysis of its Strategy and Development', *British Journal of Education and Work*, Vol. 1 (1), pp. 1-31.

Raffe, D. (1988a) 'Modules and the Strategy of Institutional Versatility', in Raffe, D. (Ed.) *Education and the Youth Labour Market*, Falmer, Lewes.

Raffe, D. (1988b) 'Going With the Grain: Youth Training in Transition', in Brown, S. and Wake, R. (Eds.) *Education in Transition: What Role for Research?* Scottish Council for Research in Education, Edinburgh.

Raffe, D. (1989a) 'Making the Gift Horse Jump the Hurdles: The Impact of the TVEI Pilot on the First Scottish Cohort', *British Journal of Education and Work*, Vol. 2 (3), pp. 5-15.

Raffe, D. (1989b) 'Longitudinal and Historical Changes in Young People's Attitudes to YTS', *British Educational Research Journal* Vol. 15 (2), pp. 129-139.

Raffe, D. (1990) 'The Transition from School to Work: Content, Context and the External Labour Market', in Wallace, C. and Cross, M. (Eds.) *Youth in Transition: The Sociology of Youth and Youth Policy*, Falmer, Basingstoke.

Raffe, D. and Smith, P. (1987) 'Young People's Attitudes to YTS: The First

Two Years', *British Educational Research Journal*, Vol. 13 (3), pp. 241-60.

Raffe, D. and Willms, J. D. (1989) 'Schooling the Discouraged Worker: Local-Labour Market Effects on Educational Participation', *Sociology*, Vol. 23 (4), pp. 559-81.

Rapoport, R. and Rapoport, R. N. (1975) *Leisure and the Family Life Cycle*, Routledge and Kegan Paul, London.

Rauta, I. and Hunt, A. (1972) *Fifth Form Girls: Their Hopes for the Future*, HMSO, London.

Reid, I. (1978) *Sociological Perspectives on School and Education*, Open Books, London.

Rindfuss, R. R., Swicegood, C. G. and Rosenfeld, R. R. (1987) 'Disorder in the Lifecourse: How Common and Does it Matter', *American Sociological Review*, Vol. 52 (6), pp. 785-801.

Roberts, K. (1968) 'The Entry into Employment: An Approach Towards a General Theory', *Sociological Review*, Vol. 16 (2), pp. 165-84.

Roberts, K. (1973) 'An Alternative Theory of Occupational Choice', *Education and Training*, August/September, pp. 310-11.

Roberts, K. (1975) 'The Developmental Theory of Occupational Choice: A Critique and an Alternative', in Esland, G., Salaman, G. and Speakman, M. *People and Work*, Holmes McDougall, Edinburgh.

Roberts, K. (1983) *Youth and Leisure*, George Allen and Unwin, London.

Roberts, K. (1985) 'Youth in the 1980s: A New way of Life', *International Social Science Journal*, Vol. 37 (4), pp. 427-440.

Roberts, K., Duggan, J. and Noble, M. (1982) 'Out of School Youth in High Unemployment Areas: An Empirical Investigation', *British Journal of Guidance and Counselling*, Vol. 10 (1), pp. 1-11.

Roberts, K., Dench, S. and Richardson, D. (1986) *The Changing Structure of Youth Labour Markets*, Research Paper No. 59, Department of Employment, London.

Roberts, K. and Parsell, G. (1989) 'The Stratification of Youth Training', *ESRC 16-19 Initiative Occasional Paper*, No. 11, City University, London.

Roberts, K., Siwek, M. and Parsell, G. (1989) 'What Are Britain's 16-19 Year Olds Learning?', *ESRC 16-19 Initiative Occasional Paper*, No. 10., City University, London.

Roberts, K., Campbell, R. and Furlong, A. (1990) 'Class and Gender Divisions Among Young Adults at Leisure', in Wallace, C. and Cross, M. (Eds.) *Youth in Transition: The Sociology of Youth and Youth Policy*, Falmer, Basingstoke.

Ryrie, A. C. (1983) *On Leaving School: A Study of Schooling, Guidance and Opportunity*, Scottish Council for Research in Education, Edinburgh.

Salaman, G. (1981) *Class and the Corporation*, Fontana, Glasgow.

Sarup, M. (1982) *Education, State and Crisis: A Marxist Perspective*, Routledge and Kegan Paul, London.

Scottish Education Department, (1983) *16-18 in Scotland: An Action Plan*, SED, Edinburgh.

Seabrook, J. (1982) *Unemployment*, Paladin, St Albans.

Seale, C (1985) 'Young People on the Youth Training Scheme in Further Education: a Survey of the First Year', *Educational Review*, Vol. 37 (3), pp. 241-50.

Sharpe, S. (1976) *Just Like a Girl*, Penguin, Harmondsworth.

Sinfield, A. (1981) *What Unemployment Means*, Martin Robertson, Oxford.

Springhall, J. (1983) 'The Origins of Adolescence', Youth and Policy, Vol. 2 (3).

Springhall, J. (1986) *Coming of Age: Adolescence in Britian 1860-1960*, Gill and Macmillan, Dublin.

Stafford, A. (1981) 'Learning Not To Labour', *Capital and Class*, No. 15 (Autumn) pp. 55-77.

Stewart, A., Prandy, K. and Blackburn, R. M. K. (1980) *Social Stratification and Occupations*, Macmillan, London.

Super, D. E. (1968) 'A Theory of Vocational Development', in Hopson, B. and Hayes, J. *The Theory and Practice of Vocational Guidance*, Pergamon Press, Oxford.

Tanner, J. (1991) 'Reluctant Rebels: A Case Study of Edmonton High-School Drop-outs' in Ashton, D. N. and Lowe, G. (Eds.) *Making their Way: Education, Training and the Labour Market in Canada and Britain*, Open University Press, Milton Keynes.

Thurow, L. C. (1975) *Generating Inequality*, Basic Books, New York.

Tomes, N. (1988a) 'Changing Certification: Vocationalism and the New Curriculum', in Raffe, D. (Ed.) *Education and the Youth Labour Market*, Falmer, Basingstoke.

Tomes, N. (1988b) 'Scottish Surveys Since 1977' in Raffe, D. (Ed.) *Education and the Youth Labour Market*, Falmer, Basingstoke.

Training Agency (1988a) *Youth Training News*, No. 50, November.

Training Agency (1988b) *Youth Training News*, No. 46, May.

Training Agency (1989a) *Youth Training News*, No. 55, June/July.

Training Agency (1989b) *Youth Training News*, No. 57, October/November.

Training Agency (1989c) *Youth Training News*, No. 56, August/September.

Training Agency (1989d) *Youth Training News*, No. 53, March.

Tuchman, B. (1980) *A Distant Mirror*, Balantine Books, Westminster, Mass.

Turner, R. H. (1961) 'Modes of Social Ascent Through Education: Sponsored and Contest Mobility', in Halsey, A. H., Floud, J. and Anderson, A. C. *Education, Economy and Society*, Free Press, New York.

Turner, R. H. (1964) *The Social Context of Ambition*, Chandler, San Francisco.

Tyler, W. (1977) *The Sociology of Educational Inequality*, Methuen, London.

Wallace, C. (1988) 'The Social Construction of Youth in History'; Paper presented to the British Sociological Association Annual Conference, Edinburgh.

Walsgrove, D. (1987) 'Policing Yourself: Social Closure and the Internalisation of Stigma', in Lee, G. and Loveridge, R. (Eds.) *The Manufacture of Disadvantage*, Open University Press, Milton Keynes.

Warr, P. B. (1987) *Work, Unemployment and Mental Health*, Oxford University Press, London.

Watts, A. G. (1983) 'Skill Transfer and Post-YTS Realities', *Lifeskills Teaching Magazine*, Vol. 2 (2) pp. 13-16.

Wells, W. (1987) 'The Relative Pay and Employment of Young People', in Junanker, P. N. (Ed.) *From School to Unemployment*, Macmillan, London.

West, M. and Newton, P. (1983) *The Transition from School to Work*, Croom Helm, London.

Westwood, S. (1984) *All Day Every Day: Factory and Family in the Making of Women's Lives*, Pluto, London.

White, M. and McRae, S. (1989) *Young Adults and Long Term Unemployment*, PSI, London.

Willis, P. (1977) *Learning to Labour*, Saxon House, London.

Willms, J. D. and Kerr, P. (1987) 'Changes in Sex Differences in Scottish Examination Results Since 1975', *Journal of Early Adolescence*, Vol. 7 (1), pp. 85-105.

Wrigley, N. (1985) *Categorical Data Analysis for Geographers and Environmental Scientists*, Longman, London.

Yancey, W. L. (1980) 'Intervention as a Strategy of Social Inquiry: An Exploratory Study With Unemployed Negro Men', in Zurcher, L. A. and Bonjean, C. M. *Planned Social Intervention*, Chandler Publishing, Scranton, Penn.

INDEX

Aberdeen, 134
Adams, J., 75
Adelson, A., 109, 113, 117
adolescence. 2, 4. 108, 139
Ainley, P., 65, 67
America, 3, 4, 113
Anderson, J. G., 111
apprentices, 2, 3, 45, 49, 57, 61, 62, 123, 129, 135, 142, 148
Aries, P., 2
arithmetic, 23
Ashton, D. N., 4–6, 8, 13, 19, 28–9, 32, 35, 37–41, 45, 58, 72–4, 76–7, 78, 85, 86–7, 88, 89, 99–100, 109, 113, 123–5, 126, 129, 142, 146, 147, 148, 151
aspirations
    general, 79
    occupational, 4, 13, 15, 61, 67, 100, 108–21, 122, 151–3, 157, 165
Ayr, 135

Bain, R. K., 111
Bakke, E. W., 75
Ball, S. J., 20
Banks, M. H., 75–7, 78, 103, 148
Bates, I., 61
Bedeman, T., 57
Bell, C., 31, 33
Bernstein, B., 19
Biddle, B. J., 3
Birmingham, 78
Blackburn, R., 94n
Borders, 134–5
Bourdieu, P., 18–19
Bowles, S., 17
Braverman, H, 73
Breen, R., 64–5
Britain, 17, 21, 28, 35, 54, 55, 65, 71, 79, 98, 155, 156
Brown, P., 31–4, 45, 109, 156, 158
Burnhill, P., 21, 25, 27
Bynner, J., 13

Cambridge Status Scale, 89, 94n, 129, 136, 164, 165
Campbell, R., 141–3
Canada, 28, 158
capitalism
    globalisation, 73, 155
capitalist society, 5, 17, 18, 67, 71, 73, 80
career
    advancement, 45
    'chequered', 85
    middle-class, 5, 8, 140
    post-school, 70
    short-term, 8
    structure, 8
Careers
    education, 111, 113
    Officers, 65, 111,
    programmes, 111–12
    Service, 113
Carter, M. P., 108, 150, 152
Census of Employment, 164
Centre for Educational Sociology, 11, 160
Chalmers, A. D., 113
class
    conflict, 6
    consciousness, 7
    domination, 6
    dynamics, 8
    inequality, 12, 23, 31, 33, 139, 152
    reproduction of, 4, 6, 7, 10, 11
    structure, 80
    struggle, 7
classless society, 7, 9, 12, 16, 17
Clough, E., 35
Cockburn, C., 59
Coffield, F., 45, 79
Cohen, P., 55
Coles, B., 28
Community Programme (CP), 84
community schemes, 57, 59
comprehensive schools, 20, 21, 23, 33
conscripts, 25, 28–9, 30, 126
'contest mobility', 34n, 113